Gifts of the Visitation

To Theresa —

Share Christ
with great joy!

Denise Bossert

"This is a little gem of a book that both women and men will return to again and again when the demands of life are such that we need fresh grounding in our appreciation of humility and grace, spontaneity and readiness, thanksgiving, and adventure and awe. It is, in two words, 'a treasure.'"

Elizabeth Scalia
Catholic blogger and author of *Strange Gods*

"Loving Mary isn't always easy for Catholics, especially converts. Sometimes the praise and adulation can seem a bit over the top. And all the various names and devotions! The 'real' Mary can sometimes get lost but, in her latest book, Denise Bossert gives all of us—converts and cradle Catholics alike—a Mary we can love through all the joys and sorrows of our lives. In *Gifts of the Visitation*, Bossert has written a book that will touch your heart and grace your soul by combining prayerful insight and meditation with the experience of one who has actually walked in the footsteps of Mary."

Woodeene Koenig-Bricker
Author of *365 Mary*

"*Gifts of the Visitation* is a fresh look at one of the most important moments of Mary's life—the Visitation—adeptly written through the personal experiences and meditations of a proficient and perceptive author. Denise Bossert takes you home, to Elizabeth and Zechariah's house, where the Christ and the Baptist meet for the first time."

Marge Fenelon
Author of *Imitating Mary*

"*Gifts of the Visitation* not only imaginatively chronicles Mary's joyful meeting with Elizabeth, it also unwraps nine gifts that encourage would-be evangelizers to grow in their Catholic faith and in their zeal for bringing it to others."

Pat Gohn
Author of *Blessed, Beautiful, and Bodacious*

"*Gifts of the Visitation* helped me to see Mary and Elizabeth in a new light and to better understand and cherish my role as Christ Bearer. It motivated me to pray fervently for an increase in these invaluable gifts, some of which I have in spades, and the others . . . not so much."

Diana von Glahn
Coproducer and host of *The Faithful Traveler* on EWTN

"In *Gifts of the Visitation,* author Denise Bossert tells a tender yet poignant story about Mary and Elizabeth and their phenomenal journey of faith, hope, and love. Bossert shares her own story, too, and, through reflection points, takes the reader by the hand, and invites them on a compelling prayerful journey."

Donna-Marie Cooper O'Boyle
EWTN host and author of *Rooted in Love*

"Denise Bossert uses the seemingly simple and oh-so-familiar Scripture story of Mary's visit to Elizabeth to take us on a journey deeper into the heart of Mary, deeper into the heart of our faith, and deeper into the untouched recesses of our own restless hearts. *Gifts of the Visitation* is a gift in itself to all those who want to grow closer to Jesus through Mary."

Mary DeTurris Poust
Author of *Cravings*

"A compelling, profound, and poetic meditation on the spiritual dimensions of the Visitation, enlivened and made uniquely present by incorporating the author's own personal experiences of each of the nine 'gifts' drawn from Mary and Elizabeth's deep encounters with God."

Helen Hull Hitchcock
Founder of Women for Faith & Family

"Denise invites us to journey deeper into the mystery of the Visitation and to activate the same gifts Mary and Elizabeth were given in order to manifest Christ in our lives today. Denise writes with such ease that reading her work feels like sitting down over a cup of coffee to receive wise counsel from a trusted spiritual friend. This book is scriptural, historical, wise, and spiritually challenging. Whether you are a cradle Catholic, new to the faith, or simply exploring, Denise breaks open the Visitation in a novel way to enlighten, edify, and even entertain."

Lisa Schmidt
Catholic speaker and writer at *ThePracticingCatholic.com*

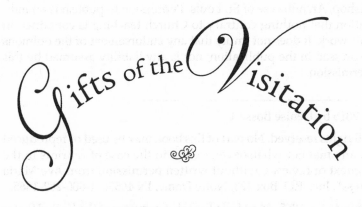

Gifts of the Visitation

Nine Spiritual Encounters with

Mary and Elizabeth

Denise Bossert

Ave Maria Press AVE Notre Dame, Indiana

In accordance with CIC 827, permission to publish has been granted on August 5, 2014, by the Most Reverend Edward Rice, Auxiliary Bishop, Archdiocese of St. Louis. Permission to publish is an indication that nothing contrary to Church teaching is contained in this work. It does not imply that any endorsement of the opinions expressed in the publication; nor is any liability assumed by this permission.

Founded in 1865, Ave Maria Press is a ministry of the United States Province of Holy Cross.

www.avemariapress.com

Paperback: ISBN-13 978-1-59471-568-6

E-book: ISBN-13 978-1-59471-569-3

Cover artwork © by Rose Walton.

Cover © www.stocksy.com.

Cover and text design by Katherine Robinson.

Printed and bound in the United States of America.

Library of Congress Cataloging-in-Publication Data is available.

FOR

MARY ELIZABETH KREMSKI

Contents

Contents

Foreword

One of the greatest blessings in my work as a Catholic talk show host is the privilege of leading pilgrimages to a number of holy sites around the world. While my favorite place on the good Lord's green earth happens to be the Eternal City of Rome and the country of Italy, I would have to say that a close second is the Holy Land. Like Rome, the Holy Land is one of those places you can visit over and over again, each time experiencing something unique and different. The churches and landmarks might be the same, but the spiritual insights change as one grows in his or her relationship with God.

During my nearly a dozen pilgrimages to the Holy Land I have had the opportunity to spend time in the very place where the Visitation occurred: the town of Ein Kerem just outside Jerusalem. The church of the Visitation stands high on the hillside overlooking the valley and quaint town below. The steep walk up-hill to this beautiful, serene location challenges even the most athletic of travelers but is well worth the effort for a number of reasons. The surrounding area is peaceful and breathtakingly beautiful, but it is the holiness of this hilltop space that grabs you when you finally completely the trek upward. One of the first spiritual experiences described by many of visitors, including myself, stems from the journey that pilgrims make on foot year after year. When you reach the summit you're sweaty, a bit tired, and out of breath, and then it hits you: How did a very young and very pregnant Mary make this journey on her own two thousand years ago? Ein Kerem is about four and a half miles from the Old City of Jerusalem. But Mary was from Nazareth, eighty-eight miles from Jerusalem. It takes nearly two hours to get from Nazareth to Jerusalem by car, so imagine how long it took Mary on the back of a donkey. It's a humbling question to ask yourself as you're standing outside the Church of the Visitation. Each time I go to Ein Kerem I have a deeper appreciation for the sacrifice Mary made and the risks she took to be with her cousin Elizabeth. I also appreciate Mary's determination. We don't see her journey described in great detail in Scripture, but she had to be a tough little Jewish girl to endure such a strenuous journey.

Another gift of the Visitation for me has been becoming more aware of the gifts of sacrifice and friendship. When you begin the tour of the Visitation site, the first thing you come to before entering the actual church itself is a courtyard and a stunning statue of Mary greeting Elizabeth. On the walls of this courtyard are forty-two large ceramic tablets. The tablets bear the words of the Magnificat in different languages. For me, having the statue next to the words of the Magnificat in a larger-than-life form speaks volumes about Mary's understanding of the blessings in her life and how she needed to be a blessing to others. I received a deeper understanding of the Blessed Mother's soul magnifying the greatness of the Lord. Mary had good reason to stay home back in Nazareth. No one would have questioned such a decision from a pregnant young woman, especially two thousand years ago. As a matter of fact, although it is not mentioned in the Gospels, no doubt given the dangers that could happen on such a long journey Mary probably did more than just raise a few eyebrows when she decided she needed to be with her cousin. But when you are touched by God, truly touched at the depths of your soul, your response is one of thanksgiving and praise. You have a desire to give back and help others as a way of responding to God's grace. The sacrifices become gifts of gratitude.

Having been to the site of the Visitation is one of the reasons I was interested in reading this book; it is also why I felt compelled to write the foreword. Thanks to my travels, I have experienced the gifts of the Visitation physically and spiritually. Every time I read the first chapter of St. Luke's Gospel I am transported back to Israel. I think you will experience the same thing as you begin to turn the pages of this book. Think about the gifts you have received in life and the lessons to be learned from the Mother of God and St. Elizabeth. And even if a trip to Ein Kerem isn't in your foreseeable future, use *Gifts of the Visitation* as a spiritual journey, a lectio divina that will transport you back to one of the holy places where our faith began—a place that continues to shower us with gifts of love, compassion, and commitment if we have eyes to see and ears to hear.

Teresa Tomeo
September 19, 2014

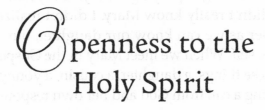

INTRODUCTION

Openness to the Holy Spirit

When I was a child, Mary was only mentioned during Advent—although we didn't call it Advent during the years my dad was a Wesleyan (Protestant) minister. In all those years, Mary existed primarily in the context of the Christmas play the children put on every year—a local version of *The Best Christmas Pageant Ever*. All the girls wanted to be Mary—from the preacher's daughter (me) to the daughter of the guy who worked in Waterloo at the John Deere factory to the daughter of the farmer

who kept my family supplied with fresh milk and eggs
year-round.

Mary came to me in bits and pieces in those years
before I entered the Catholic Church. She was there next
to the donkey with the broken ear in the Nativity set: a
girl dressed in blue in the Christmas pageant. During my
college days, I saw her as the subject of a Michelangelo
sculpture or a painting by Titian, Rubens, or Raphael.

I don't remember when I heard the word *Visitation* for the first time. It was probably when I became
Catholic and began praying the Joyful Mysteries. Before
that, I didn't really know Mary. I didn't realize we can
know her as we can know our daughter, our sister, or
our very self. When we meet Mary in the Gospels, she is
all of these things: a daughter, a cousin, a young woman
discerning a call from God and her own response to that
call.

To know Mary, we must be able to imagine Mary's
inner monologue after the Annunciation when an angel
tells her she will bring Jesus into the world. We need to
begin to hear Mary speak, to sense what she was feeling,
to understand her growing desire: *I must go. I must tell
someone. I must see my cousin Elizabeth.*

As we journey with Mary, we get a sense of her
mind working as she ponders the angel's words, as the
Magnificat—a prayer, a revelation—is imprinted on her
soul and pours forth when she reaches Elizabeth and
Zechariah's doorstep, words familiar to us: *My soul proclaims the greatness of the Lord!*

We learn to listen to Mary as Elizabeth did, and we
learn to embrace Mary as Elizabeth did. Why is this so
important? Because Mary is God's game changer, his

pièce de résistance. Mary whispers to us, *Come and learn from me. Watch me. Feel what I feel. Desire what I desire. Risk everything as I risk everything. Share Jesus Christ as if it's what you were born to do—because it is what you were born to do.*

In the deepest part of the Christian soul, we know this. We know that we are tied to the hills of Judea where Mary encountered Elizabeth. The hills of Judea became God's first mission field; Mary, the first missionary; the Visitation, the blueprint for sharing the Gospel message.

There is a miraculous dimension to what transpired between these two women—and to all encounters that are made possible by the power of the Holy Spirit. The relationships themselves are pregnant with grace. They have the potential to bear Christ to the world today.

Which specific gifts of grace were present at the Visitation? And if we welcome God into our relationships as Mary and Elizabeth did, will we have access to these same gifts?

The answer is yes. We will realize that every gift we have been given in the natural order is really a gift from God. We will also receive gifts in a superabundant way—gifts of grace that go beyond what we have been given by way of our DNA. But there is even more to it than that. The Visitation gives us a glimpse into what it means to activate those gifts in such a way that *we give birth to Christ* in the world today. Pause there for a minute, and consider the words you just read. If we invite God to be in our midst, if we are open to receiving the gifts that were present at the Visitation, we can bring Christ to our world and to those we encounter each and every day.

Quite simply, the Visitation is the key to sharing Christ with the world right now, in our families, places of employment, schools, communities, and parishes. If we open our hearts fully to God's presence, if we are willing to say yes to him completely, if we are ready to embrace the nine gifts described in the chapters of this book—the very gifts which Mary and Elizabeth embraced—then we will also share Christ with the world. Christ will come to us and be born anew in our own circle of influence. In his General Audience on November 6, 2013, Pope Francis used the phrase "a communion of charisms" and explained that charisms are gifts or particular graces that are given to some for the good of many.[1] A communion of gifts (or charisms) is an excellent description of what was shared at the Visitation. And the gifts present at the Visitation are meant for us as well. They are meant for our good and for the good of those we encounter.

In the book *Mary, the Church at the Source*, Pope Benedict XVI writes, "Only a conversion to the sign of the woman, to the feminine dimension of the Church, rightly understood, will bring about the new opening to the creative power of the Spirit, and so to Christ's taking form in us, whose presence alone can give history a center and a hope."[2]

This prophetic word is not just for women. It is an invitation to each of us to enter into that feminine dimension of the Church. To do that "rightly" as Pope Benedict describes, we will need a perfect model to emulate. And for that, we have only to sit at the feet of Mary and Elizabeth and learn from them.

Here, we see two women with one goal. They simply wanted to bear Christ to the world. St. Maximilian Kolbe understood this goal. He founded the Militia Immaculata and boldly proclaimed that their mission "was nothing less than to bring the whole world to God through Christ under the generalship of the Immaculate Conception, and to do so as quickly as possible."[3]

✳ We are being sent into the world to bring Christ to those we meet, and our success depends upon the degree to which we permit Mary's example to challenge us. When we first meet Mary and Elizabeth in the Gospels, they are in the middle of improbable and overwhelming situations. They could have looked at their circumstances and decided they couldn't be bothered with anyone else's needs—spiritual or physical. Had they been shortsighted, concerned only with their own lives, families, and pregnancies, they would have missed the purpose of their call. Here is the paradox: their improbable situations uniquely *suited them* for the work before them. Incredibly, God chooses to show up in our improbable moments, transforming even the messiest and most tragic life event into a divine visitation.

All of us are given improbable situations, and each one provides a frame for our acceptance of and entrance into the gifts that might arise as a result of our openness to our "visitations." For me, that acceptance and entrance began in 2003, when my father passed away. For a while, I was so consumed by grief that my grief almost eclipsed God's larger purpose.

In those early weeks after his death, I began searching for answers to my questions about suffering, and I started that search by delving into the boxes of books I had inherited from my father's personal library. In the bottom of one box, I found a copy of St. Augustine's *Confessions*. Augustine said the happy man is the man who seeks the Lord. As I read those words, I became open to whatever God wanted to show me, give me, or even take *from* me.

It was a time of grace. I did not realize that my openness to the gift of grace would enable me to become a Christ-bearer. Honestly, I didn't even know I was called to this mission, and I had a very limited understanding of the word *grace*.

About two years before my father died, we chatted over lunch, and he began talking about death and eternity. His candor that day emboldened me, and I asked him a question that I had wanted to ask for many months. "Dad, do you remember Elijah and Elisha? I feel as if we are connected like that, and I was wondering, inasmuch as you are able to do it, would you leave me the 'double portion' like Elijah left for Elisha?" I wasn't even sure what I meant by that. All I knew was that I hoped to be given that double portion.

Later, I would read St. Louis de Montfort's *True Devotion to the Blessed Virgin* and begin to understand the meaning of the words "double portion." This saint helped me to connect the dots between Mary, a path to holiness, and the double portion. "All [Mary's] domestics, that is, all her servants and slaves, are clothed with the double garments, her own and those of her Son."[4]

This is the double portion I had asked to receive without realizing what I was asking my Protestant preacher-father to send me. Dad's reply was immediate, though he had no more idea what I meant than I did. He said yes.

On a Sunday in December 2003, my father passed away unexpectedly from a pulmonary embolism. This was it. This was the life event that would throw open the doors to a divine visitation. That season of grief became my hills of Judea, a place where God would visit me and make all things new.

Within weeks, I discovered *Dark Night of the Soul* by St. John of the Cross. The book helped me process the theology of suffering. By the time I finished reading that book, I knew the author I wanted to read next. If St. John of the Cross could help me sort through things that had happened to Dad, then maybe his spiritual companion would have something for me. I went in search of a book by St. Teresa of Avila. I remember the day that I was sitting up in bed reading her book *The Interior Castle*. I put the book down on the bed and stared at it. Everything in me said, "I want what she had—what both she and St. John of the Cross had."

Then the realization washed over me: *To have what they had, I would have to become part of the same faith that gave birth to that kind of holiness.* I had to become Catholic.

These two Carmelite saints, who had lived five hundred years ago, shared their own visitation experience with me. They had somehow visited me through their writings, calling me to come and follow. Through them, God was *visiting me.*

As Mary was drawn to travel to the hill country of Judea, I felt drawn to the Carmelites. But I did not know where to begin. Mary knew how to get to Elizabeth's house, but how did one find Carmelite saints who lived five centuries ago? One could not simply travel through time to a small village in Avila, Spain, and have a chat with the saints. Yet I had so many questions about how to begin the journey of conversion to the Catholic faith shared by these saints and where it all might end.

In July of that year, on the Solemnity of Our Lady of Mount Carmel, I saw a woman by the name of Mary Elizabeth Kremski on EWTN's *The Journey Home* program. (For those who are prone to see the hand of God in all things, note the name of the woman: Mary Elizabeth.) I was not in the habit of watching Catholic programs. I had simply been changing channels at random. I stopped immediately when I saw the name of the guest, because the words written next to her name said that she was a Third Order Carmelite. I jotted a set of questions down and mailed a letter to the show, and they forwarded it to her. A beautiful letter arrived in August 2004 from Mary Beth. The next month I began RCIA class, with Mary Beth as my spiritual mentor.

I was right where I needed to be in order to experience every gift of grace God wanted to pour out upon me. It all depended on one prerequisite, a kind of predisposition. Both Mary Beth and I had to bring an openness to the journey, a readiness for anything, in order to embrace whatever God had in mind for us. We had to be all-in, holding nothing back, offering him a total gift of self. The foundation for every gift of the Visitation is a spirit of openness to God's divine will.

To know how to do this, to fully understand what it means to have an openness to the Holy Spirit that makes us ready for a divine visitation, we can look to the women who exercised the gifts that were given in the first Christ-centered friendship of all time. Mary and Elizabeth became the quintessential model of women who understood their dignity in the eyes of God and embraced the roles God had given them to share Christ with the entire world.

Like Mary, we are called to hold nothing back, to be ready to give God a *total* gift of self no matter what situation we may find ourselves in—whether we're pregnant or we've just buried a parent, whether we are in a happy marriage or our marriage is falling apart, whether we are starting college next month or preparing to retire. Man or woman, each of us is called to say the prayer, "God, I'm yours. Use what you can. Lead where you will."

Mary and Elizabeth's witness is meant for us in this moment of time. Like them, we are to become Christ-bearers.

Mary's openness to God's plan unleashed nine gifts that ushered in the birth and ministry of God's Son: spontaneity, courage, joy, readiness, humility, adventure, hospitality, wonder and awe, and thanksgiving. These are the gifts we see in action in those early days of the Gospel story. By activating these gifts in our own lives, Jesus Christ will be born anew in the lives of those around us. And it all begins with an openness to God's plan. So, even if you are in the middle of your own chaotic or cataclysmic life event, it is time to simply say, "I'm ready. I'm ready for whatever God wants to show me, give me, or even take from me. I am wholly at his disposal, and I am ready to give birth to Jesus Christ in my corner of the world."

CHAPTER ONE

𝒜 Spirit of Spontaneity

In May 2014, I traveled to Israel and prayed at the Basilica of the Annunciation in Nazareth. This beautiful church is built over the dwelling where Mary lived. Like the homes of other families of Nazareth, Mary's home would have been very simple, perhaps with only one or two rooms—hardly more than a cave in appearance, with an outdoor gathering space just beyond the front door. Somewhere on the right side and in the top third of that door, there would have been a mezuzah attached to the door frame. When I was in Israel, I noticed that there is a mezuzah affixed to the door frame of every Jewish home and hotel room to this day.

The mezuzah is a piece of wood, metal, or stone containing a parchment scroll with the Shema (passages from Deuteronomy) handwritten on one side and the name *Shaddai* (meaning "mighty and all-powerful One") written on the back. All Hebrew people were familiar with the Shema:

> Hear, O Israel, the Lord is our God, the Lord is one. You shall love the Lord, your God, with all your heart, with all your soul, and with all your resources. And these things that I command you today shall be upon your heart. And you shall teach them to your children, and you shall speak of them when you sit in your house and when you go on the way, when you lie down and when you rise up. And you shall bind them as a sign upon your arm and they shall be an ornament between your eyes. And you shall write them upon the doorposts of your house and on your gates. (Dt 6:4–9)

These verses would have been watchwords for Mary. She would have recited them and lived by them. They would have formed her, and the Lord would have surely used these verses to prepare Mary for the moment for which all of Israel had waited—the moment when she was given the choice to say yes to God's plan for her to become the Mother of the Messiah.

These words would have prepared her to have a spirit of spontaneity because they directed her heart and mind toward total devotion to the Lord. They would have formed her to give an immediate assent regardless of the manner in which God asked her to serve him. This spirit of spontaneity is the first gift we will explore in our journey to the Visitation, and the Shema is the pathway to this gift.

If you are a person who loves God "with all your heart, with all your soul, and with all your resources"— as the Shema instructs—you will be a person who is ready with an immediate yes when God calls. The gift we receive through recitation of the Shema is the gift of spontaneity—a heart after God's own heart, a will conformed to his will, and hands and feet willing to serve.

As we look to the example of Mary, we realize that we are being called to read the words of the Shema and embody them, letting them draw forth a spirit of spontaneous cooperation in our hearts as well. Go back to that text and read the words carefully and prayerfully. If you wish to pray a novena as you read these nine chapters, you can find a novena and the Shema at the end of the book (see appendix). The novena will assist you in praying with Mary for a greater outpouring of these gifts. Each chapter will end with a prayer, which can either conclude the chapter's reflection or serve as a beginning to the day's novena. The chapters and the novena will help you to step into Mary's world and begin to think as she thinks, love as she loves, and share Christ as she shared him with the world.

But who is this young woman from Nazareth? Who is the maiden that lived by the Shema? How can we begin to see her with our mind's eye? To know her heart? To feel what she felt? The Song of Songs (Song of Solomon) offers us a good place to begin. These lines from the Old Testament speak prophetically of Mary:

> A garden enclosed, my sister, my bride,
> a garden enclosed, a fountain sealed!

A garden fountain, a well of living water,
streams flowing from Lebanon. (Sg 4:12, 15)

Mary is that enclosed garden, which no man has ever touched. She is the Ark of the New Covenant, the Daughter of Zion, the sister of all Hebrew people. She is the bride which the Spirit of the Lord overshadows. She is the fountain where water is first sanctified and made holy by the power of the Holy Spirit. She is the New Eve. And it is to this woman that the angel appears.

We know from Luke's gospel that the angel approached Mary with great respect, saying, "Hail favored one" (Lk 1:28). For a moment, Mary was concerned. What did this greeting mean? The angel set her at ease, assuring her that all was well. "Do not be afraid, Mary, for you have found favor with God. Behold, you will conceive in your womb and bear a son, and you shall name him Jesus. He will be great and will be called Son of the Most High, and the Lord God will give him the throne of the house of Jacob forever, and of his kingdom there will be no end" (Lk 1:30–33).

While most young women would fixate on the promise that her son would be a king, that the Most High would give that son dominion over the entire world, and that this kingdom would never end, Mary does not focus on the glory that would come by way of her Son. Instead, she considers her call to holiness—and that is all.

How can this be, she asks the angel, if she is to remain pure, chaste, a woman who has never known a man? Holiness is her only concern. "The Holy Spirit will come upon you," the angel responds, "and the power of the Most High will overshadow you. Therefore the child to be born will be called holy, the Son of God. And behold, Elizabeth, your relative, has also conceived a son in her old age, and this is the sixth month for her who was called barren; for nothing will be impossible for God" (Lk 1:35–37).

And here is the moment of truth: Will she respond with a spirit of spontaneous assent? Will she activate the gift of spontaneous cooperation that has been cultivated by the words of the Shema and protected by a life dedicated to God? The whole world waits. What will this young woman of thirteen or fourteen years say?

Would she worry about the ramifications of her response? Would she ask for a little time to consider the possible fallout before accepting God's offer—ramifications such as getting stoned to death by a community that would not understand? Would she mention Joseph, perhaps ask Archangel Gabriel to give Joseph a prophetic word or two to ease things along before having to break the news to him? And while the angel was at it, could the angel find a way for her parents to be there for the little angelic visit so as to prepare them as well?

Would Mary tell the angel that she wanted to do the will of God but that she felt conflicted? If the angel could get all of Nazareth behind it, maybe then it would make sense. Maybe *that* would be the sign that she should say yes. Sure, God had sent an angel to her, but he couldn't have thought that would be enough to raise the scandalous to the miraculous in the minds of family and friends.

Are these the things Mary pondered? No. Mary voiced none of these fears, though she certainly had reason to fear. Instead, Mary responded freely and spontaneously, with a faith and acceptance of divine will

unmatched by any other human. She did not doubt.
She did not barter. She did not hesitate. We see a spirit
of spontaneity in her response that challenges us:
"Behold, I am the handmaid of the Lord. May it be done
to me according to your word" (Lk 1:38). This was her
response after one very brief conversation with God's
holy messenger.

Imagine the heavenly choirs in that moment. The
enemy would be taken down by the yes of this young
woman. In the moment the Spirit overshadowed Mary,
in the moment God's own Son took on human flesh, the
Father must have been laughing. Yes, God must have
laughed. Even today, God delights in us when we meet
challenges, both big and small. Even today, God waits
for our yes and takes delight in our spontaneous cooperation with grace. It all echoes back to that first yes.

This was the beginning. A spiritual coup was taking
place, and the rightful king would take back his kingdom all because a young woman said yes to God.

Let us lift the veil for just a moment on a little village in the hills of Judea—over eighty miles south of
Nazareth—where Elizabeth is already waiting for us.
Sacred scripture does not tell us about the moment Elizabeth realized she was pregnant with John the Baptist,
the forerunner to the Messiah, and so we must use our
imaginations. Elizabeth has been waiting a long time to
give her yes to childbearing. And now the childbearing
years have passed. It seems that she has been asked to
give her assent to another plan: a life without a child.
Elizabeth has quietly accepted this call. She and her husband, Zechariah, have turned their hearts fully to God—
to a holy life of service and to a quiet life of fidelity to

God. But with an instantaneous assent to God's divine will, she receives the gift of new life. She embraces the miracle. Nothing will ever be the same again. And to this, Elizabeth says, "So be it." Somewhere in the hills of Judea, an old woman gives her "yes," and she waits for whatever God wants to do next.

Mary and Elizabeth gave themselves completely to God's divine providence—no second thought required.

We tend to think that it is better to be skeptical of new ways of thinking and to resist changes in our plans for the future. We cling to our ideas stubbornly. We have to be knocked down by some pretty tough stuff before we will consider a change in direction. Oh, we are so different from Mary! Yet daily, we are called to spontaneously and completely give ourselves to God and to offer our spontaneous yes—regardless of how our assent might change our lives.

In 2003, I experienced that "control-alt-delete." My life was about to change completely, and I gave my yes to the whole thing. It was as deliberate as holding down the three keys simultaneously: control, alt, delete.

When I was younger, I would not have picked up a book by any Catholic saint because I was raised as an evangelical Protestant. I listened to contemporary Christian music, I read contemporary Christian books, and I looked to contemporary Christian figures. My worldview was Protestant, and I clung to that. But my father's death changed me. I needed answers to a whole new set of questions, and I looked for answers wherever they could be found. I still turned to the familiar source for wisdom: my father's deposit of books, since I could no longer go to him directly. By the time I had finished

reading Augustine's *Confessions* from Dad's personal
library, as well as John of the Cross and Teresa of Avila
from my nearest bookstore, I was ready to let God teach
me more about this ancient Church.

A couple of years before Dad died, he mentioned
a priest by the name of Fr. Larry. Dad said he really
liked this priest and that Fr. Larry was on the ministerial
board in town with my father. Dad was not in the habit
of praising Catholics or Catholic theology, so his words
stuck with me.

In June 2004, I felt nudged to call Fr. Larry. Talk
about acting spontaneously! Yet it seemed as if contact-
ing this Catholic priest might be the next step in my faith
journey. I told Fr. Larry I was feeling an inexplicable
tug toward the Catholic Church. He didn't seem that
surprised.

My dad's Catholic friend told me that everything
comes down to what I believe about Holy Communion
and Our Lord's words in the sixth chapter of John's Gospel. If I could accept Jesus Christ at his word, I would
continue this faith journey. If I could not believe in the
Real Presence of Jesus Christ in the Eucharist, the journey would come to an end right there.

St. John of the Cross and St. Teresa of Avila had
brought me to Christ—to Jesus Christ in the Eucharist.
For me, it was a personal visitation. Now I had a decision to make.

Eucharist. The word alone sounded strange to me.
It felt as if I was back in first-semester Spanish class,
attempting to roll my *r*'s for the first time. *Eucharist.* I
said the word out loud.

Did the Lord really say that bread would become his body, something divine, Christ himself? I wasn't sure. It would take a monumental leap of faith to believe something outside my realm of knowing. But I was willing to listen to discover if God said it was true. I opened my Bible and read John 6: "Amen, amen, I say to you, unless you eat the flesh of the Son of Man and drink his blood, you do not have life within you. Whoever eats my flesh and drinks my blood has eternal life, and I will raise him on the last day. For my flesh is true food, and my blood is true drink. Whoever eats my flesh and drinks my blood remains in me and I in him" (Jn 6:53–56).

The Holy Spirit had prompted me to call Fr. Larry. I had received a word of advice from the priest, and I had acted upon it. I had read the passage in the Gospel. I was seeking Christ and all he had for me, and it motivated me to cooperate with the movements of the Spirit. My response wasn't the spontaneous yes of Mary. It was methodical. It was tentative. But when I read Jesus' words in John 6, I knew as surely as if God's messenger were standing in the room with me and passing along a word from God: "Unless you eat the flesh of the Son of Man and drink his blood, you do not have life within you. My flesh is real food, and my blood is true drink."

In that moment, I accepted something I had never considered: Jesus Christ wanted to come to me. He wanted to be within me. He wanted to abide in me and I in him—to touch the world I touched, see the world I saw, and move among the people I knew.

I could say yes, or I could say no. Saying yes would mean everything would change. Saying no would mean

my life would keep going along familiar paths. I was
ready to say yes to God.

What is God saying to you? Is there something he
has spoken into your heart, something he wants you to
embrace? Has he come to you in a personal way and
invited you to make a decision of your own?

Mary's response was immediate even though it
meant her life would never be the same. Her response
was unwavering and unrestricted. She gave her full
cooperation. She didn't make bargains with God. She
didn't worry about how she would raise this child or
what Joseph would say. She didn't spend time dwelling
on the fact that women who were found pregnant outside of marriage were typically stoned to death in her
culture. She didn't even ask what would happen if she
said no. Her spontaneous and full cooperation opened
the door for the Holy Spirit to do the greatest work of
all time.

Elizabeth, too, responded swiftly to God's plan
with her full cooperation. Talk about a control-alt-delete
on life! Nothing would ever be the same for Elizabeth
and Zechariah. And to that, they said, "Amen. So be it."

We are being called to respond to God in a similar
way: with a full yes, a complete embrace, and a spontaneous assent.

REFLECTION

Am I ready to abandon self-will? Am I ready for total
self-donation to God? What things might I be holding
too tightly? My plans? My hopes? My words? Am I

willing to say yes, without question or reservation, with the same spirit of spontaneous cooperation that Mary and Elizabeth had? What is God proposing to me right now?

Lord, give me a spirit of spontaneity. Imprint the Shema on my heart. Teach me to be docile to your will, to be quick to obey your word, and to offer a spontaneous "yes" the moment I hear you speaking to me. I bow my will to your will. May this offering pass through the loving hands of your Mother. And may she, in turn, show me how to bear you to the world. For your glory. Amen.

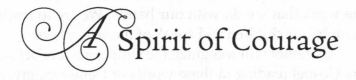

CHAPTER TWO

A Spirit of Courage

In chapter 1, we learned that the verses of the Shema are nearly as old as the Hebrew people. The ancient words helped to mold the twelve tribes of Israel into God's holy nation, and they prepared Mary for her response at the Annunciation. Let's look again at the core verses of the Shema:

> Hear, O Israel, the Lord is our God, the Lord is one. You shall love the Lord, your God, with all your heart, with all your soul, and with all your resources. And these things that I command you today shall be upon your heart. And you shall

23

> teach them to your children, and you shall speak
> of them when you sit in your house and when
> you go on the way, when you lie down and when
> you rise up. And you shall bind them as a sign
> upon your arm and they shall be an ornament
> between your eyes. And you shall write them
> upon the doorposts of your house and on your
> gates. (Dt 6:4–9)

In these verses, we read that we are to bind the
words from Deuteronomy on our arms and on our fore-
heads—keeping them in our mind and living them by
the work that we do with our hands. We are to teach
them to our children and speak of them to others.

Catholics will recognize the simple gesture before
the Gospel reading in these words of Deuteronomy: a
cross on our forehead, a cross on our lips, and a cross on
our hearts. We make this gesture as a promise to keep
the Gospel story in our minds, pondering what we hear;
to keep it on our lips so that we might be quick to share
it with others; and to let it burn with zeal in our hearts,
affecting how we live and what we do with our hands.
It is a promise to remain faithful in our thoughts, words,
and actions even in the face of fear—even when our
courage is tested.

Like the gesture before the Gospel reading, the Sign
of the Cross also has seeds of the Shema in it. Through
the Sign of the Cross we bind ourselves to Christ, and we
bind his words to our hearts and lives. We draw upon
these promises when we feel afraid, when we need to
be courageous for Christ. For this reason, you will see
Catholics making the Sign of the Cross *precisely* in the
moments they feel afraid: at the site of a car crash, as

their plane lifts off the runway, when they feel overcome by temptation.

The Shema. The Gospel gesture. The Sign of the Cross. These all become ways of saying, *God owns this battle. I will not be afraid.*

The spirit of courage is the second gift we will study in our journey to the Visitation. Mary learned from the patriarchs and matriarchs who came before her. We see the faith and trust of Abraham and Sarah in Mary's response to Archangel Gabriel. We recognize the courage of Judith and Queen Esther in Mary's yes in the face of possible death. She is Naomi and Ruth, who trusted God as they journeyed from Moab to Israel. But there is something more here. She is the handmaid of the Lord, and her courage is unparalleled. No one in biblical history can match the *fiat*—the yes—of Mary, for she was a girl, barely a woman. She did not have a husband leading the way. She did not have Israel standing behind her when she gave her yes. While she is like the spiritual giants of the Old Testament, her courage even surpasses theirs.

We must not forget that she was a real girl and that salvation came to us by way of her yes, by way of her womb. She was not an angel. She was not God. She is one of us—and she was barely beyond the age of a child. And yet, she conversed with an archangel and gave her *fiat*—even though it would change everything.

It's important to grasp even a little of what it took for her to keep her feet planted on that ground when she realized a real angel was sharing a real message from God. After she gave her *fiat*, she traveled courageously through dangerous hills—without her family, without

Joseph, without support or protection from anyone—to
visit Elizabeth who lived in the hill country of Judea. I
have been in those hills. I have climbed a few of them.
This was no easy journey. It would have taken Mary
at least four days to cover the more than eighty miles
between Nazareth and Elizabeth's home in Judea. Yet,
Mary heads for Elizabeth's home with great haste without her parents, without Joseph, without any defender
or protector—except the Lord.

In order to understand the degree of courage it took
for her to set off for Elizabeth's home, we must remember what it was like to be a young teenager—but utterly
alone. Her only protection was the God of the Shema.
She had him firmly fixed in her mind, on her lips, in her
heart. And now, she had him within her womb.

She didn't have AAA insurance or a high-
performance car. She didn't have a wallet full of money
and credit cards. She didn't have state police or airport
security to ensure her safety. She simply had faith and
a whole lot of courage to travel between Nazareth and
the Judean village of Ein Kerem where Elizabeth and
Zechariah lived.

Mary's courage is unprecedented. In order to grasp
the degree of courage at play here, it's helpful to recall
who we were at that young age.

I remember what I was like at Mary's age. And I
was not ready to meet any angels. My preacher-dad
always waited until nightfall to realize that he'd left
his Bible on the podium at church. He'd casually lift
his eyes from a bedtime snack to tell me, "Why don't
you run down to the church, Sis, and get my Bible for
me?" I'd roll my eyes and say, "Dad," adding a couple

of syllables to the word as I said it. I wasn't usually
disagreeable with my dad. But the idea of going into a
church at night—by myself—sounded more like a good
way to run into an angel.

And the last thing I wanted to meet was an angel.

But Dad would continue to prod me out of my
chair until I gave him a reluctant "okay" and trudged
down the road to a darkened church.

Once inside, I would suddenly shift gears, dashing
full speed through the narthex, to the wall on the other
side (where a nutty electrician had decided to place the
switch plate), where I would frantically feel along the
wall for light switches, the whole time praying, "Please,
no angels. Please, no angels." Then, I'd run like a maniac
to the platform. Finally, Bible in hand, I'd run back down
the aisle, hitting the light switch in one fluid motion, as
I passed through the narthex and out the church doors.
I would barely drop the pace as I headed for home with
the Bible tucked under my arm. When I handed the Bible
to Dad, he'd say, "Well done," which always left me with
a surge of pleasure and a sense of relief that the little
mission was over. Then, we would all head off to bed.

That's how I felt about meeting angels when I was
fourteen.

Not Mary. Mary was asked to walk down a difficult road. She was asked to hold a conversation with an
angel. She was given the opportunity to bear Christ to
the world, but only at the risk of losing her own life in
the process.

At some point, we must realize that God is asking
us to follow as Mary did, to walk down a few dark roads
of our own. He asks us to enter his Church and receive

the Word Made Flesh and take Christ into our homes and places of work—as freely as Mary received Christ into her womb and shared Christ with others.

On those evenings when my father asked me to run down to the church and get his Bible, I would roll my eyes and hope that he would let that Bible sit on the podium overnight. How many of us roll our eyes when God asks something of us? How many of us say, "Not there, not me, not now."

Mary was fully human. She felt as we feel. But her response was different. She responded with courage.

Once again, let us peek into the home of Zechariah and Elizabeth. Let us skip across the hills from Nazareth of Galilee to Judea and climb that final hill to the village of Ein Kerem. Can you imagine the amount of courage required of Elizabeth to embrace pregnancy in old age, to anticipate delivering and raising a child when she and Zechariah were senior citizens, to face the people of their community once her body began to show signs of pregnancy? Add to all of this uncertainty and confusion the fact that Elizabeth now has a husband who cannot speak. Zechariah went into the Temple to pray, and he returned to her unable to say a word. We cannot know how much Elizabeth was able to piece together when Zechariah returned, but certainly she longed to hear her husband share all that had transpired when he prayed before the Lord. Yes, Elizabeth, too, was being called to walk courageously with God.

Before we brush the story aside and say Mary and Elizabeth's courage has nothing to do with us because we go to Mass, we remember holy days of obligation, we go to confession regularly—we do what's required of us—let's realize that we are all called to follow in the footsteps of Mary. Every faith journey requires moments of courage. If you haven't been courageous for Christ, you probably aren't fully stepping into the gifts of the Visitation.

To be open to whatever God wants of *us*, we should respond with an eager and spontaneous yes when God reveals his plan. And then, we can put on the mantle of courage and follow through on our promise to God.

How does one get the gift of courage? Where is the door to this gift? Does one need to pray the Shema or meditate on some scripture?

Oh, my friend, this gift is already yours. You may not realize it. You may not have ever activated it in your life, but you already have the gift of courage.

From the moment the bishop sealed you with the Holy Spirit at your Confirmation, you have been the beneficiary of the gifts of the Holy Spirit: wisdom, understanding, right judgment, courage, and so on. It does not matter if you are naturally brave. It has nothing to do with your DNA. In the Sacrament of Confirmation, you were given the gift of courage. You have only to pray and ask the Holy Spirit for the manifestation of this gift.

But even before that—even before you were baptized—God came to you and led you to himself. You had just enough grace to find your way to the sacraments. So, even then, there was just enough courage to help you find your way. And that is how it was for me.

In September 2004, I joined RCIA classes. It was six months after I read the Carmelite saints and two months after I saw Mary Beth Kremski on television. I met with

Shawn Mueller, the RCIA instructor at my parish, and he handed me annulment papers and told me to fill them out and return them when they were completed. My first and only thought was whether I could complete the forms without anyone in my family knowing. The annulment process was a Pandora's box. Opening it was a very bad idea. I was divorced. I was remarried to a wonderful man. And I wanted everything to stay neatly ordered.

But Shawn had said that it would be good for me—healing, he said.

I had held the papers nervously and replied, "I know. That's what your parish priest just told me." What could a priest and a happily married man know about bad first marriages anyway? That's what I wondered.

I had walked into the church that day and told the secretary that I felt a strange desire to become Catholic. Learning from Mary, I was ready to give God my yes. Then, I was hit with the annulment papers, and my courageous resolve left me stranded. I went home and dropped the annulment papers in my desk drawer and decided I would worry about the annulment thing if I made it through RCIA without any insurmountable hang-ups.

My parents had raised me to know that Jesus must become the most important person to me and that following him meant going wherever he would lead and doing whatever he gave me to do.

But there I was, in the parish office of a Catholic church. I had found Jesus in the Eucharist, and nobody else in my family agreed with my reading of the Gospel of John, chapter six. For them, it was grape juice and cubed bread. What mattered was what we felt in our hearts. That was evangelical Protestant theology.

Now that I believed in the Real Presence, I would never again see the Lord as offering mere bread and wine. It was Christ, and I *longed* for him. And if it meant sitting through RCIA class—or filling out those annulment papers—then that's what it meant.

But first, I would address some of the issues that remained.

I say "some" of the issues. Really, there was only one: Mary.

In December 2004, Shawn introduced the class to the Church's teaching on the Immaculate Conception. I announced to the entire class that I couldn't accept that Mary was conceived without sin. I was willing to admit that Protestants had let the pendulum swing too far in the opposite direction, relegating Mary to a minor role in the Christmas story, but I felt that was in response to excessive Catholic Mariology. I explained that, while I believed the Lord could do that for Mary, I was convinced it was highly unlikely that he *did* do it. And at that moment, I didn't even have enough faith to say, "I believe; Lord, help my unbelief."

The terrible thought hit me then. Where does one go when she believes in apostolic succession, the papacy, purgatory, the Communion of Saints, and all Catholic teaching *except* the Immaculate Conception?

After many attempts to help me understand, Shawn mentioned that I could place a petition before the Blessed Mother. If I had sincerely given myself to the task of understanding and I still couldn't embrace this teaching, he told me, I could always ask Mary to show me the truth.

I went home and wrote out a petition to Mary. As an evangelical, I had placed many petitions before the Lord. That was not a new concept. And I didn't have a problem with asking Mary to answer my petition. I just didn't think she would do it.

A lot was riding on this petition. The Immaculate Conception was also the one obstacle that stood between my father and the Catholic Church. In fact, if he could have resolved this issue, I'm convinced he would have converted to the Catholic Church. Before I made my petition to Mary, I prayed, "Lord, I will follow you wherever you lead, even if it is down a road my father could not take. I just want to get this right. And so, I beg you *not* to answer the petition I place before your Mother if this teaching shouldn't be embraced." Then I turned my heart to Mary and laid it on the line. Among the words that I wrote were these lines:

> Mary, if you are as the Catholic Church says, and if you love me, please answer this petition. I want someone to communicate with me by your inspiration. Mary, I want the message to come from you to the ears of one who could know no other way. Please choose someone who, for me, would represent the universal Catholic Church. Then I will know I am right where I am supposed to be and that the Church's teachings are *all* correct, terra firma, especially the teachings about you. Please answer my petition before the end of the year—I know, that's just two weeks.

"It's unlikely that I will receive a response," I thought, "almost as unlikely as the Immaculate Conception."

But I was willing to follow, wherever God led me. I was willing to say yes no matter what was demanded. Some may say that embracing the teaching on the Immaculate Conception is not a big deal. Some may wonder why that took courage. But it took all my courage. My parents believed it to be a false teaching. If the petition was answered, I would know it was true—and I would walk away from the only vestige of Protestant teaching that remained an obstacle to my full conversion to the Catholic faith. And the difficulties would not end there. If I continued the faith journey and the annulment was not granted—if my first marriage was determined to be a sacrament—then I would have some difficult decisions to make. Somehow, I would have to explain to my new husband that I wanted to live as brother and sister, raising our daughter together but not sharing a marriage bed—all because I hungered to receive Jesus Christ in the Eucharist.

It didn't come to that. The annulment was granted. The first marriage was found to be non-sacramental, and my second marriage (to John) was eventually blessed and convalidated by the Church. But God put me to the test. I had to be all-in. I needed the Holy Spirit to give me a very large portion of courage.

And so, I made a petition to Mary on a Sunday afternoon in December.

And I waited.

Following Jesus Christ takes great courage. Our Lord knew this, which is why he said, "In the world you will have trouble, but take courage, I have conquered the world" (Jn 16:33). Where do you suppose the child Jesus heard these words for the first time? Did he hear them from a mother who told him her own story of courage? Her courage was strong at the moment an archangel appeared; in the days to follow, as she pondered the message; and when she thought about what she should do next—where she should go, who she should tell. Mary was a woman of great courage, and a young Jesus would have witnessed that spirit of courage given in full measure by the Holy Spirit to his own Mother. Some thirty years later, he would exhort his followers to be courageous, for he had dominion over all things. No weapon formed against them would prosper. No principality or power of darkness would overcome them. He had conquered the world.

Theologian George Weigel says that the challenge of sharing Christ "cannot be met by timid or lukewarm Catholicism," but instead, we must propose "the Gospel in a compelling and courageous way."[1] In short, we must be courageous, like Mary.

Courage doesn't just happen. We have to will it, want it, and be open to it. It is a gift we have been given from the moment we were sealed with the Holy Spirit and the bishop anointed our forehead with sacred chrism. But we have to activate that gift. How do we do this? We pray, *Come, Holy Spirit. Come, with the gifts you have given to me.* And then, by the power of the Holy Spirit, we have to face our greatest fears and lay them down. It can't matter what others say. It can't matter what they will think. We must resolve to act when the Lord calls us to action, to speak when he gives us the words to say, and to set aside everything for the sake of the kingdom.

ℛEFLECTION

How can I begin to follow Christ more courageously? Am I ready to respond to my calling even if others will not understand? What is my greatest fear? Am I ready to lay that fear down once and for all? What can I do today to activate the gift of courage that I received when I was confirmed?

Lord, manifest a spirit of courage within me. Through the power of the Holy Spirit, and the anointing I received at Confirmation, fill me with a spirit of courage. Give me the resolve to act when I must act, to speak when I must speak, and to set aside my own fears. I promise to follow the path marked out for me. I give everything to you— including my fears. May this offering pass through the loving hands of your mother. And may she, in turn, show me how to share you with the world. For your glory. Amen.

CHAPTER THREE

A Spirit of Joy

With spontaneous and courageous assent, Mary embraced the Father's divine plan. The prophetic Word—the hope of the world—was living and growing within her womb. She had never known the intimacy of the marriage bed, and yet this miracle surpassed every miracle the world had known: a virgin had conceived God's Son!

In the handful of nights that she stayed at her home in Nazareth before going to see Elizabeth, she must have placed her hand over her womb and dreamed about this child. What would he be like? Would he look like her? Would the boy know all these things—how the angel spoke to her and what he had said—without her telling the child any of it? Or would she whisper these amazing things to him as he sat on her knee? Would she share them with him as she tucked him in at night? "You are a gift from God, my Son. The whole world has waited for you for a very long time. You are precious, holy—heaven's little lamb."

A gift of the Holy Spirit is joy. Indeed, joy flows abundantly from faith, hope, and love. And Mary embodied these three theological virtues perfectly. Mary also carried God within her womb—God *himself*!

From the moment Mary was overshadowed by the power of the Holy Spirit, her soul filled with the gift of joy. God was all around her and within her, and his presence yielded joy.

Every prophet in Israel since ancient times knew he would come. Every scholar of Sacred Scripture had studied the text. And every prophetic word was distilled down into a little life, barely the size of a mustard seed—living and growing in Mary.

Mary was the chosen handmaid, Israel's daughter, the virgin of prophecy. She would give the world a savior. The words of the prophets must have swirled around her. One after another, the sacred texts arose in her heart to praise God with her and through her: "Sing and rejoice, O daughter Zion! See, I am coming to dwell among you, says the Lord" (Zec 2:14).

As Mary replayed the conversation with Archangel Gabriel in her mind, as she went about the day's chores, the sun shining on her face, the wind blowing the hem of her garments, her heart must have filled with joy. Her own heart was giving humanity to God's Son. Even now, his Sacred Heart was forming within his little body in the quiet, dark, immaculate womb of Mary.

And yet, he was sustaining her life as he had from the moment of her own conception. Giving *to* her, he was now receiving *from* her. The mysterious intimacy between the Immaculate Heart and the Sacred Heart goes back to this moment, in which Mother and Son first communed with one another in the quiet shadows of a Nazareth twilight, in the early rays of the morning sun, in the darkest part of the night when everyone lay sleeping. In the two thousand years that have passed since the Incarnation, we still struggle to grasp this divine mystery. What was it like for Mary, who had only known a few days that the Son of God was living and growing within her womb?

He had come, that their joy might be complete—her joy, her parents' joy, the joy of Nazareth and of Jerusalem. Even the joy of Elizabeth and Zechariah in the hills of Judea—yes, even their joy was made complete *because of this little one.* Marian theologian Edward Sri makes the connection between joy and the words of Sacred Scripture when he points out that Mary went "in haste" to see Elizabeth. "Mary's going in haste points to her joy over what God is accomplishing in Israel and in her own life by sending the Messiah-King."[1] The joy of the Annunciation manifested itself in Mary's desire to go "in haste" to visit her relative.

It is time to turn our thoughts more fully to those hills, to the town of Ein Kerem—a town that means the "Spring of the Vineyard"—where Elizabeth, too, is filled with joy. Two angelic visits have carried the news of Elizabeth's pregnancy—not one, but two! First, the

angel told Zechariah that his wife would bear a son who
would be the prophet of the Most High God. And then,
an angel confirmed the pregnancy to Mary, saying that
even her relative Elizabeth was in her sixth month, for
nothing is impossible with God. Yes, Elizabeth, who
was deemed too old to bear a child, is pregnant as well.

In 2013, I researched the symptoms of premeno-
pause and perimenopause. I am getting close to that
season of life, and I wanted to know what I could expect.
The most interesting results from my research did not
come from medical sites but from forums where women
shared their stories. One forum in particular grabbed
my attention. A number of women shared their symptoms—symptoms that could mean they were entering
menopause, but symptoms that *also* mirrored those of
early pregnancy. And, contrary to what most people
think, these women were excited about the possibility
of a pregnancy late in life although they knew those
same symptoms were more than likely due to hormonal
changes of menopause. Some of these stories stand out
in my memory—such as that of the woman who had
never had a child and had long ago accepted that it
would never happen.

Now, she wondered. Could it be possible? The ten-
derness of her breasts, the missed periods, the queasi-
ness—was she pregnant, after so many years? What an
amazing thought! Just when she least expected it, could
she now be pregnant?

What was it like for Elizabeth? For Elizabeth, menopause had come and was now long gone. There was
no chance for pregnancy—except from God, for whom
nothing is impossible. What was it like to feel the breasts

preparing to feed, the body preparing to deliver, the child learning to kick and stretch within her womb?

If I had been Elizabeth, I would have asked Mary over and over, "What did he say? When he told you I was in my sixth month, how exactly did the angel say it? He told you that you would conceive the Son of God— and then he spoke of this child? My child? Oh, Mary, and to think I was sure my joy could not grow beyond what I already feel! And here you are, traveling all this way to tell me what an angel said! Blessed are you—for you believed the angel's words! Blessed are you for coming all this way just to share your joy with me!"

Elizabeth had spent the first six months of the pregnancy unable to converse with her husband, for he was made mute. The angel had said that Zechariah would not speak again until their child was born because he had doubted God's prophetic word. Elizabeth must have yearned to hear Zechariah speak to her and to share what the angel had said. She must have yearned to hear him describe what it was like to encounter God's holy messenger. But when Mary stepped across that threshold and called out to Elizabeth, the Holy Spirit reached out and anointed John the Baptist, sending him leaping in Elizabeth's womb—and the joy of the Lord was multiplied. Mary had arrived. And after that initial embrace, Mary began telling Elizabeth what Zechariah could not say.

Generation after generation, women have shared the joys of pregnancy with one another, but surely, there has never been more joy over new life than the joy shared between Mary and Elizabeth in the hills of Judea.

But all good things can be tainted with evil, and joy is certainly one of those very good things that can be damaged or destroyed by the evil one. The surest way to lose our joy is to succumb to jealousy. Mary might have wished that she had a husband with whom to share the journey. During her three months in Ein Kerem, Mary had a privileged view into Zechariah and Elizabeth's marriage. It might have made her wish that God had talked to Joseph as he had Zechariah, so that from the first moment of the Annunciation she would have had the companionship of a husband who might share this amazing pregnancy with her. Even so, she had a spirit of joy, and she let nothing steal that joy from her.

And what about Elizabeth? How easy it might have been for Elizabeth to resent Mary! Elizabeth might have wanted to focus on herself and her own pregnancy. She might have felt that Mary's child took away the fullness of her joy. She might have thought Mary could never be as delighted over pregnancy as Elizabeth was because new life came to the young woman without heartache, without anticipation, and without years and years of waiting. For Elizabeth, it had been a dried-up dream— an almost-forgotten longing. And now, God had remembered her.

Elizabeth might have wanted to bask in that truth and think only of her own blessing.

Sure, Elizabeth was experiencing a miraculous pregnancy, but Mary's pregnancy was divine. Elizabeth's little boy would one day say of Jesus, "He must increase; I must decrease" (Jn 3:30). The reality of that future dynamic existed even now. But Elizabeth's joy, like Mary's, was made complete *because God had chosen them for unique roles.* There was a kind of complementarity in their pregnancies and their individual roles in bearing Christ to the world. And they fully embraced one another's vocation. The Holy Spirit had infused Elizabeth with the supernatural understanding that this was the Mother of *God.* And Elizabeth received that word—joyfully!

As a student in RCIA class, I struggled with Marian theology. The fact that I have written a book about Mary is a miracle in itself. For forty years, I did not permit the Blessed Mother to play any part in my faith life. I didn't think I had anything to learn from Mary's role in the life of Christ. The Christological synergy that existed between Elizabeth and Mary was lost on me.

I kept Mary at a safe distance from my life as a disciple—something that now seems absurd. But that is how it was for me until the year I converted. I am not exaggerating when I say that I almost did not become Catholic *because of Mary!* My bias ran very deep.

But I loved Jesus in the Eucharist, and I wanted to receive him. And that is the only reason I went to Mary and asked her to send me a sign that would settle all of my doubts about her.

The day after my petition to Mary, I received a letter from the woman who had appeared on EWTN's *The Journey Home* the previous July. As I said in the previous chapter, I presented the petition to Mary on a Sunday. I received the answer to that petition the next day—the very first opportunity for mail delivery.

I had not heard from Mary Beth since August. But in December 2004 she wrote me a second time to encourage me to keep going. Her letter was dated December 8,

2004. Above the date, she had hand written "The Feast of the Immaculate Conception" (Solemnity). With tears streaming down my face, I read her two-page, single-spaced letter.

I had been ready to abandon the journey. Unlike Elizabeth, I had not welcomed Mary with joyous ease the moment I came face to face with her in RCIA class. But the Holy Spirit came with a mighty rush as I opened that letter, as my eyes saw the date and read the Marian title so carefully written above the printed date.

Understanding pulsed through me as it did Elizabeth the moment an unborn John the Baptist kicked within her womb. "I know who she is! She is the Immaculate Conception."

That letter sealed everything for me. Like St. Thomas when he touched the wounds of our Lord, my doubts were gone instantly.

From that moment on, I knew it was so: Mary is my mother. And like the truest mother, she loves me and knows me better than I know myself. That letter left Scranton, Pennsylvania, before I had my Immaculate-Conception meltdown in RCIA class, and it arrived at my home west of St. Louis, Missouri, one day after my petition to Mary. Our Lady proved herself to be the Immaculate Conception and a mother with impeccable timing.

The next day, I walked into the parish office and asked to talk to Shawn, my RCIA instructor. I sat down and laid the envelope on his desk. "Okay, Shawn. Mary is the Immaculate Conception." God visited me through Shawn and Mary Beth, and I would never be the same again.

Wherever two or three are gathered in his name, God promises to be there. In that moment, we experience a divine visitation. Every year, RCIA instructors open the door for a divine visitation when they shake the hands of their new students and welcome them to the journey that will lead them to the Eucharist. Every time a priest opens the door and waits in the confessional, the priest is making room for a visitation. Every time a diocese serves the poor, or welcomes the homeless, or stands with the forgotten, or speaks for the voiceless, it ushers in a visitation. Every time we meet together and pray the Mass, we are preparing our hearts for a divine visitation; we are preparing our hearts for a joy that is meant to be shared with the world.

Yes, the joy we bring to these moments is contagious. The gift of joy is multiplied.

More often than not, these visitations come cloaked as day-to-day life. We pick up a pen and write a letter. We send an e-mail, make a phone call, visit a friend. We get in our cars and drive to Mass on Sunday morning. We serve the poor, teach our children, pray the Rosary. All of these are moments of divine visitation. These are the hills of Judea for you and me. They become an opportunity for us to journey to Ein Kerem, the "Spring of the Vineyard," where we are the bearers of the Gospel message. Pope Francis says a missionary is one who "knows the joy of being a spring which spills over and refreshes others."[2] We must be that joy-filled spring. Yes, we are the "Spring of the Vineyard," an Ein Kerem in the world.

During his address at the Mass of Ordination and Installation in the Diocese of Marquette, Bishop John

F. Doerfler exhorted the faithful, "Be a friend of Jesus, make a friend, and introduce your friend to Jesus."[3] And then, he put the faithful on the spot, asking them, "Do you accept this invitation?" The faithful responded with a powerful "I do." Bishop Doerfler replied, "Wonderful. That'll keep us busy 'til Christ comes again in glory!" With those words, St. Peter Cathedral in Marquette, Michigan, filled with applause and laughter. It filled with joy.

Our souls respond to the call to share Christ with that same exuberance and joy. We are called to eagerly embrace those moments in which God touches another person through us. The Holy Spirit infuses these moments with joy, a joy that springs from the Incarnate Son, visiting us by way of the Immaculate Heart of Mary. Like John the Baptist, we leap for joy. Like Elizabeth, his mother, we shout with gladness.

It all harkens back to that first moment, when two women embraced. Their unborn babes communed. And the Spirit of the Lord danced among them. The gift of joy that God had given to them was shared, and the sharing of the gift made the gift grow.

REFLECTION

Is my life marked by the spirit of joy? How can I share my joy in deliberate ways with others? Through writing cards? Through stopping by a friend's house or leaving a joy-filled message on a friend's voicemail? Do I try to make one act of shared joy a part of what I do every day? When joy seems to elude me, do I call upon the Holy

Spirit to fill me with joy as he did the Blessed Mother and St. Elizabeth? Do I focus excessively on the experiences in life that mute or even snuff out joy? Would I like to invite the Holy Spirit into my life so that my soul is fertile ground for the gift of joy? Where in my daily prayer life can I add that simple invitation: "Come, Holy Spirit, fill me with a spirit of joy"?

Lord, give me a spirit of joy. Lead me into a deeper walk with you. Reveal more of the Father's love for me. And let me have a share in the joy of following you. Show me the path I must walk—the path that yields joy. I am ready for whatever you have planned for me. Let your mother journey with me, holding my hand when I need it, wrapping her mantle around me when joy seems elusive. Let her joy be my joy as we share you with the world. For your glory. Amen.

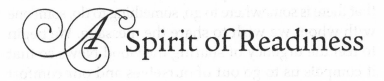

CHAPTER FOUR

A Spirit of Readiness

As Mary rested in her bed those first few nights after the Annunciation, as she replayed in her mind those things the angel had said, it is likely that she realized that the key to what she must do next was embedded in the angel's words. Mary knew how to interpret the hand of God. It wasn't a hunch. She wasn't trying to out-guess God. She walked closely with the Lord and rightly anticipated what God wanted her to do.

Every event, every word, every movement of the Holy Spirit—she pondered all of it—and it was like a finger pointing her now toward the hills of Judea. A spirit of spontaneity had called forth courage, the spirit

49

of courage had yielded joy, and the joy provided the necessary strength that made her ready for travel. Cardinal Donald Wuerl describes the one who shares Christ with others as one who has "boldness or courage, connectedness to the Church, a sense of urgency, and joy." As we have seen, these are Mary's trademarks. Moreover, Cardinal Wuerl connects the urgency to the Visitation, saying, "We need to see in Luke's account of Mary's visitation of Elizabeth a model for our own sense of urgency."[1]

Down to our very core, like Mary, we sense that that there is somewhere to go, something to do, someone with whom we wish to share the message. We begin to feel the urgency of sharing the Good News so that it compels us to go out of ourselves and our comfort zones. Catholic writer Marge Fenelon reminds us that "there was a reason [Gabriel] told her about Elizabeth's pregnancy, and Mary knew that. . . . She understood the angel's news as a call to action."[2]

A spirit of readiness is the fourth gift we will look at together, and we see it clearly activated as Mary considered the angel's words: "And behold, Elizabeth, your relative, has also conceived a son in her old age, and this is the sixth month for her who was called barren; for nothing will be impossible for God" (Lk 1:36–37).

As Mary contemplated these words, it is likely her heart filled with a profound desire to see Elizabeth. Joy fills, and then it sends—that's how it always works. The joy of the Lord seeks to go beyond itself and spill over to another. It always demands expression. It simply cannot be met with a yawn. The joy of the Lord never elicits the apathetic response, "Isn't that nice."

The joy of the Lord *is* the mandate. It *is* the sending. The joy of the Lord drives the mission—by design. Mary would have hungered to see Elizabeth. She probably shared that desire with the Lord, asking him to open the necessary doors if it was his will for her to go to the hill country of Judea.

Everything in her may have wanted to see Elizabeth, but this was no easy journey. The picturesque town of Ein Kerem is located more than eighty miles from Nazareth. If Mary traveled in the cooler season, she may have journeyed through the Jordan Valley. If she traveled during the summer, the heat may have required her to travel over the mountains where she was not in familiar territory. Samaritans might cause trouble, as well as thieves waiting for the unsuspecting or those traveling alone. This was not going to be an afternoon stroll.

Once Mary knew what God was asking her to do, once she knew what that "next thing" would be, Pope Francis tells us, "she does not loiter, she does not delay, but goes 'with haste.'"[3] God revealed himself to her. And then he prompted her to share the gift with another. He even laid the groundwork for her journey. Yes, long before the apostles went on mission trips, Mary was sent to the first mission field in the hills of Judea. Before St. Paul shared the Gospel story in foreign lands, Mary shared the Gospel story with Elizabeth and Zechariah at Ein Kerem.

Once filled with Christ, she acted on what she had received. And this is a call for us as well. There are many ways to share the Gospel, as we will see in the next few chapters. Sometimes, we share the joy through practical assistance—giving to another in the name of Christ.

Sometimes, we step in the gap and intercede—taking another's needs before God in the name of Christ. Sometimes, we open our mouths and share the gift with our words—lifting and exalting the name of Christ.

Here we meet the Shema all over again. It's the gesture before the Gospel Acclamation. I will dwell on the Lord with my mind, I will speak of the Lord with my lips, and my love for the Lord will burn with holy zeal so that I will praise him with the work of my hands. My whole life will be a journey to bring the Gospel to others, and the joy of the Lord will be our strength. Joy fills. God sends. We act.

So often, our own faith journeys follow this pattern. God sends, but he does not reveal everything all at once. We are asked to act, to move in faith. As we make an initial act of faith, we begin to understand what the next act of faith will be. The Lord leads us along the journey step by step, always giving us the opportunity to accept his unfolding will. If we have a spirit of readiness, we keep saying yes to God. Catholic speaker Kelly Wahlquist says these are the moments in which Mary invites us to become part of her *fiat*, instantly extending her *fiat* so that it becomes our *fiat* as well.[4]

In that moment, we take our place under Mary's mantle. In that moment, the Holy Spirit ignites a fire within us. And we are ready for whatever may come. These moments are not always filled with sunshine and rainbows. Sometimes, these moments do not resemble anything we may have imagined for ourselves.

Grief sent me on a journey for answers to the question of suffering. The Carmelite writers I discovered in that season of mourning prompted me to explore

Mother Church. By the time I entered the Church, I was already writing a monthly column for my diocesan newspaper. One act of faith led to another. And within a year of reading those first books by the saints, I was a syndicated Catholic columnist. By the time I had been Catholic for six months, my column in *The St. Louis Review* had been picked up by newspapers of the Archdiocese of Oklahoma City, the Archdiocese of Dubuque, the Diocese of La Crosse, the Diocese of Wichita, and the Diocese of Juneau. These papers had a combined circulation of more than 200,000. God was sending me out to share Christ in ways I could not have imagined.

Sometimes, our mission takes us through river valleys, where we have nourishment and peaceful days. For me, diocesan writing was like the peaceful journey along the Jordan. Sometimes, we journey through the mountains where the steps are difficult and danger surrounds us. I passed through the rugged hills when I conversed with my husband on topics of faith. He remained hostile toward many Catholic teachings, and our conversations about faith often ended in arguments about Mary and Church authority. I struggled to find my footing in those hills where I walked alone. No one in my family had made this journey. We were a family of Protestant preachers and evangelists. Nobody was Catholic—except me. This was definitely the rugged journey to Ein Kerem and not the tranquil journey through the river valley.

Freelance writing became my "next thing." The Spirit's voice urged me to go there. *That is what you must do. Leave the others to God.* The writing was my Ein Kerem. My family was a kind of Nazareth. I kept them in my heart as I followed the path God was placing before me. And I suppose Mary also carried her dear ones from Nazareth in her heart as she made her way to Elizabeth's home.

Like Mary, we learn to listen to the Spirit's call, discern what is in accordance with God's will, and then act with haste. We are called to read the signs, discern the divinely prescribed action, and then embrace the work at hand—just as Mary did. If we do not go, others will not experience the outpouring of the Holy Spirit. If Mary had remained in Nazareth, Elizabeth would have been deprived of Christ-living-in-Mary. And an unborn John would have been deprived of the Spirit that reached out and anointed him even within the womb of his mother, Elizabeth.

And so, we learn from Mary to embrace next things. With Mary as our guide, we discover what it means to have a spirit of readiness for whatever God wants to do next in our lives.

What is God calling you to now? Maybe you have heard his voice in the past, but lately, you haven't thought about what might be next in your journey. Perhaps you have lost focus or your ears are a little unaccustomed to discerning that still, small voice. What is the spirit of readiness speaking to your heart?

My second husband was raised in the Southern Baptist faith. He did not enter the Catholic Church with me. As wonderful as it might have been for my husband to go through RCIA with me, I sometimes wonder if I would have turned to writing as I did. If I had been able to share with him this great joy, the words would not have demanded another form of expression. The

desire to share with another was so strong that I had
to write—just as Mary's desire to share with one who
would understand propelled her from Nazareth to Elizabeth's home. One wonders if she would have traveled to
those hills if Joseph had been present at the moment of
the Annunciation. God works all things together for our
good, as it says in Romans 8:28—and also for the good of
those we meet when we step away from our Nazareth,
our comfortable surroundings and life as usual.

But it can be lonely.

Each of us longs to have a companion on this journey. God gave Elizabeth to Mary. And Beth became that
companion for me. By the time I entered Mother Church
on August 14, 2005, Mary Beth and I were spiritual com-
panions. We shared the complementarity of our gifts
and opened ourselves to the possibility that God had
more than one miraculous encounter in mind for us. I
sensed how much I needed Beth to guide me through
those early days of catechesis, and she rejoiced because
she had begged our Lord for a companion on her faith
journey. God saw my need and heard her petition.

In those early years, Beth encouraged me to remain
patient with my husband who was dead-set against
leaving his Baptist tradition to join me in the Catholic
Church. She counseled me to remain steady when others
were unable to understand, to be tranquil at the feet of
Jesus, and to be productive in capturing the journey in
writing.

To be sure, Mary provided Elizabeth with this kind
of spiritual companionship. God had brought them
together. Christ was at the center. Their shared journey

through pregnancy was the means by which Christ and his prophet would come to the world.

So, too, for Beth and me, Christ was at the center. Our collective journey through the world of writing would be the means by which we would share Christ with the world. Beth also interceded for me daily, offering her illness and sufferings up for me—as I am sure Elizabeth did for Mary. Pregnancy can be difficult—especially when one is older. I know this from personal experience. My first pregnancy was incredibly easy; the last was incredibly difficult. We can be confident that everything Elizabeth experienced in her advanced age was a gift she rendered to God with gratitude for the ultimate gift of Jesus Christ.

My friend Beth has suffered from lupus for many years. In spite of the illness, she never complained. She barely mentioned it, except to say that she was offering it to Jesus for his will to be done in all things. Over time, I pieced together the degree of her suffering. There were times she turned down invitations to travel and be a guest on Catholic shows. I knew how difficult it must have been to embrace the cross in moments like this.

But Beth leaned into grace even then—*especially then*. She even interceded when I was invited to appear on Catholic programs. Beth was discerning her own next thing during that time. And the call was changing. I suppose that is how it was for Elizabeth and Mary. That first Visitation brought incredible changes to their lives. For one woman, old age would be radically different than she had anticipated. For the other woman, holy virginity would take on a new, miraculous meaning.

The Lord enters into our expectations, and, so often, he reorders our lives beyond anything we could imagine. Christ was leading Beth deeper into a life of contemplative prayer. She was writing less. I was writing more. Her suffering increased. My schedule was at max capacity. We both praised God that we were being used, though differently, and learning to say, "Blessed be God forever."

God equips each of us for the work he sets before us. He uses others—in many kinds of visitations—to prepare us for our calling.

There is great benefit in reading books about the writing life and joining writers' groups, but Beth has taught me something no writing book or writers' group has ever taught me: how to trust that our Lord will use the writing if he has need of it, and how to offer it up as an offering of another kind if he chooses not to share it with others. Even articles and manuscripts that never make it to print can be a gift to God. Every spiritual writer knows that such offerings are perhaps the most sacrificial ones a Christian writer can give, but while this is something Catholic writers know, it is not something I learned from other writers, or through books on the writing life, or in a writing class. Beth taught me this during our moments of visitation.

Beth has also firmly counseled me to discern God's will, to be quick to do the work if he desires it, and to let it go when the call is over. She has taught me how to pray at all times, whether I have sufficient time for quiet contemplation or the day's schedule is double-booked. She has helped me to recognize and accept consolations

from the Holy Spirit, but not to require them in order to
remain faithful.

"It's all grace," as Beth's beloved St. Thérèse of
Lisieux says. If illness changes your plans, it's grace.
If you convert (as I did) or come back to the Church
(as Beth did), and you confound family or lose some
friends, it's grace.

Mary teaches us these things in an even more profound way. If the seasons permit a journey by the river,
it's grace. If the seasons demand a journey through the
rugged hills, it's grace. If the whole community gets
behind you, like the people of Ein Kerem did for Zechariah and Elizabeth, it's grace.

But if nobody seems to be with you, and you are
facing those first few nights in Nazareth alone, it's grace.
If Joseph does not perceive the call of God in the moment
you perceive it, it's grace. If God chooses to share his
plan with both husband and wife simultaneously as he
did with Zechariah and Elizabeth, it's grace.

Where is your journey going right now? Is it
through the rugged hills of Judea? Is it taking you along
the cool waters of the Jordan River? Is it headed toward
those who don't share your faith? Or is this a time in
which you need an oasis, an Ein Kerem—a few months
beside the "Spring of the Vineyard" where you can com-
mune with God and with a brother or sister in Christ
who can tend to your soul? Or are you headed somewhere that is a little intimidating?

Mary shows us that we are simply called to be
ready for what comes next. We must go where he leads.
His grace is sufficient for that. It is enough for what he

calls us to do, but it is not enough when we pile on our own thoughts, worries, plans, and critiquing.

Sometimes, as we discern, we must give a no in order to give God our yes. For three months, Mary gave a "yes" to Elizabeth, and she gave a "little later" to Nazareth. She gave a "yes" to God and a "God's will be done" with regard to Joseph.

Mary was always ready for next things. And today, you are that "next thing." She has waited for you—and for me—and for those dear ones that only we can reach for Christ. It is time to step beneath her mantle.

It is time to embrace whatever comes next—even if it is not what you had imagined for yourself, even if other things must wait while you give God your yes to what he has placed before you today. It is time to learn from Mary how to embrace next things with a spirit of readiness.

ℛEFLECTION

What "next thing" is God asking me to embrace? Am I willing to say yes to whatever God has planned? Am I ready to abandon complacency and apathy and exchange them for a spirit of readiness? Who does God want me to welcome into my life right now? Is there someone with gifts that will complement my own God-given gifts? Am I ready to spiritually befriend this person, fully, without jealousy, manipulation, or self-serving agendas?

Lord, give me a spirit of readiness for whatever you desire from me and for me. May all that I do— and every good thing that it might render—pass through the loving hands of your mother and be placed before you as a perfect and holy gift. May Mary, in turn, show me how to share you with the world so that I am ready always to bear you to another. For your glory. Amen.

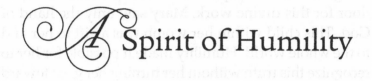

CHAPTER FIVE

A Spirit of Humility

No list describing the gifts central to the Visitation would be complete if it did not include the gift of humility. Mary was part of the lowest social strata. She was fully aware of her social and cultural status as a young Jewish woman. Spiritually, however, she was royalty—a handmaid destined to be a queen. God looked upon her lowliness and declared, "She's the one." Humbling *himself*, he took on our humanity—becoming fully man while remaining fully God—and he did this within the womb of Mary.

Mary had a résumé that only God could read. And that résumé was replete with humility *and* holiness.

Mary's humility made her fully aware of the great work that God had done and was doing within her. It did not cross her mind that she merited this favor, even though we know that God found her "full of grace." Neither did she cling to her own plans, but she submitted to the plan of God. In short, she emptied herself of her own thoughts and desires about the future, contemplating only God's abundant mercy. That's humility.

She knew that what was happening to her was a mighty work by God. While future generations would recognize that her supreme holiness provided an open door for this divine work, Mary saw only the hand of God. This child within her womb was a gift to her and to the whole world. Humility made it possible for her to recognize this truth without her turning her gaze toward herself.

It's even more amazing than that. When she looked at the possible ramifications—being ostracized by her community or being put to death by stoning—even then she embraced God's plan. Even then, she saw herself as one who had been blessed simply because God looked her way. The gift, regardless of the price she had to pay, was hers because God was good. She recognized the blessing even if it required her to lay down her own life. It is difficult to imagine that kind of humility.

Any humility I possess has come through humiliations due to weakness rather than humility that rises when a holy person humbles herself before God as Mary did. I have fallen into some of the pitfalls of the age, with all its pride. I have been prone to consider myself as growing in holiness when I sense gifts at work rather than to see them as signs of grace. Mary doesn't fall into that trap, although with her, there *was* a correlation between an outpouring of gifts and her personal holiness. She recognized God's loving hand at work. She did not consider her own merits.

Before we dismiss Mary, thinking that we are incapable of that level of holiness, we need to consider Elizabeth. Like Mary, Elizabeth is a model of humility for us. We look at Elizabeth, and we begin to realize that humility is a gift for us as well. It is not just a gift for the Mother of God. But humility comes at a price. It is a gift that comes only when we empty ourselves of self-love and pride and deliberately pursue a life of holiness. Sacred Scripture says that Elizabeth and Zechariah were righteous in the eyes of God and had observed all the commandments of the Lord blamelessly (see Lk 1:6).

Elizabeth was a matriarch—the culmination of a long line of matriarchs in salvation history. Elizabeth had a husband, and her husband had some status. We first see him at the Temple, entering the sanctuary of the Lord to burn incense to God (see Lk 1:9). Both she and Zechariah were esteemed in their community. It is true that Elizabeth was barren, and her infertility certainly lowered her in the eyes of the community, but Zechariah's love for his wife would have mitigated that humiliation to some degree. And then, Elizabeth became pregnant. Suddenly, she is raised to the highest social level at Ein Kerem—throughout the hills of Judea for that matter. And yet, she had received the gift of humility as well.

Elizabeth does not focus on her own righteousness but declares, "So has the Lord done for me at a time when he has seen fit to take away my disgrace before

others" (Lk 1:25). This is a miracle that surprises and
also delights the people of Ein Kerem. The community is
able to recognize God's hand in the miracle, and they are
able to comprehend the gift because it came in the manner they understand—by way of the marital embrace.
In the moment that Mary visits Elizabeth, Elizabeth is
at the zenith of her status in the community. And yet,
what does Elizabeth say when Mary arrives? What does
Elizabeth do when she sees Mary?

She shouts, "Blessed are you among women!"
Immediately, Elizabeth recognizes the one who has
received the greatest gift from God—Mary, who carries the Messiah. Elizabeth knows that her own blessing comes by way of Mary's child! The gift Mary has
received renders blessings for them all, for the entire
world. "Blessed is the fruit of your womb!" Elizabeth
exclaims, and she runs to Mary and embraces her (see
Lk 1:42).

The matriarch humbles herself before a young
woman. If you want to know how to love Mary, how to
venerate Mary, how to see her as God sees her, listen to
Elizabeth. Watch what Elizabeth does. She immediately
turns her face toward God, sees Mary through God's
eyes, and humbles herself, elevating Mary to the highest
position among all women. Elizabeth does not inflate
her own importance; neither does she downplay her
own gift in order to elevate Mary's gift. Elizabeth knows
that it is *all* from God. He deserves all the praise. That
humble posturing of her spirit enables her to recognize
Mary as the *most* blessed woman. This woman standing
before her, a woman their culture would castigate and

ostracize, perhaps even put to death—this woman is the *most* blessed one of all. And Elizabeth proclaims it!

As a Protestant, I did not recognize these things in Mary and Elizabeth. I knew the story well, but I had never unpacked the underlying humility at play in the Visitation. They were key women in the Nativity story—I knew that. But Elizabeth was barely mentioned, and Mary's recurring role in the New Testament was downplayed in my faith formation as a child and young adult. And I didn't spend very much time pondering this "one who was blessed among women," even though Elizabeth herself says that all generations will call Mary blessed. I never put it together that Elizabeth was the first one to recognize Jesus through Mary.

All Marian devotion comes down to this: Mary magnifies Christ. Eventually, Joseph, the shepherds, the Magi, and Simeon and Anna would all recognize Jesus in the arms of Mary, but it was Elizabeth who first saw Mary as a path to Christ. Marian devotion is rooted in Sacred Scripture—but for forty years I missed the signs completely.

I only permitted Jesus to come into my heart—just Jesus and me; there was no double portion of Jesus and Mary back then. I believed that anything more than that would take away from my love for Christ. But Mary only magnifies Christ. Like Elizabeth and Anna and Simeon, we are called to recognize Jesus in the arms of Mary, to see her as a sure and easy path to Christ.

Like Elizabeth, we are to humble ourselves and recognize Mary as the Mother of our Lord. If you want to receive the gift of humility, imitate Elizabeth as she receives Mary into her home. Let go of your own achievements. Forget your own agendas. Lose the title you have acquired.

Simply see Christ living in Mary.

When I began writing this chapter, I turned to my friends in the Legion of Mary at my parish. "Talk to me about Mary's humility," I said. "You grew up with her. You know her and her humility in ways that I have not known. What does the spirit of humility in Mary mean to you?"

They poured out their hearts. And many of the insights at the beginning of this chapter are their insights. I listened as they spoke of this one who has mothered them from their earliest days. So many times since I entered the Catholic Church, I have thought along with Elizabeth, "Who am I that the Mother of my Lord should come to me?" (see Lk 1:43). Who am I that I have access to this woman above all women? Who am I that she has come to me and called me to be her daughter in the order of grace?

While working on this book, I created a list of the gifts of the Visitation. I sent the preliminary list to my friend Beth, and she wrote back to say—with tender love—that I should consider Our Lady's humility as well. I knew she was right. No study of the Visitation is complete without a deep examination of the spirit of humility present in both Mary and Elizabeth.

If we contemplate the life of Mary without seeing her in light of her humility, we miss much of what Mary longs to teach us. There is a reason humility is at the center of this book on the Visitation. Humility is the most essential gift for those who wish to share Christ with others. It makes way for every other gift to grow and flow. If an open heart lays the foundation for God's work among us (as we read in the introduction), then humility is the cornerstone of that work. But for me, humility has been an elusive gift—one of the most difficult gifts to activate in my life.

Who are we that God would come to us? Who are we that he would visit us? Who are we that he should humble *himself* and become a man, to live and die for us? I am a sinner. In our American culture, I may be something worthy of a little acclaim: a mother, a wife, a writer, a woman with both bachelor's and master's degrees, a *magna cum laude* grad.

Maybe you have some feathers in your cap as well.

Maybe you have degrees, or a nice house, or a certain status in your community.

But in comparison to the Divine One, we are sinners. Only by his redemption are we raised to a new order—the order of grace. Our path to holiness runs straight to and through the Cross of Christ. His mercy is our only hope of salvation.

My growth in humility has come, not because of my holiness, as it did for Mary and Elizabeth, but because of my weakness. I have caused my own humiliations. I have not humbled myself as I should, but rather humiliated myself as I careened down paths that have taken me far from God's gentle plan. I have discovered humility at my own hands and through a sequence of bad decisions.

At the Visitation, we see the humility of two women who rank so much higher than the rest of us, but they *still* bow and accept God's will. They magnify God and consider themselves of low estate.

God has raised me up *despite my weaknesses.* He has given me gifts, *in spite of my brokenness.* He has called me to share his Son with others. Yes, even me. And he has called you to share Christ, too. Despite your weaknesses, in spite of your brokenness, he wants you to share in his gifts and to offer them to others.

It is a *gift from God* to be permitted to share his Good News. It means we are blessed. We have been raised so high that our lives can become living testimonies of the glory of God. Who are we that he would be mindful of us—that he would raise us up to receive him and then send us out to proclaim him? We are only able to recognize this as a gift if we humble ourselves.

An odd thing about humility is that it seems difficult to embrace until we embrace it—and then, it is sweet. It is welcomed. The American culture requires us to be so many things. God asks us to empty ourselves. The world tells us to be the life of the party—and then comes the desolation of the morning after the party. God promises us life—and then he comes that we might have life more abundantly than ever before.

We are resistant to the whole idea of humility. It seems to be such a big thing—to submit to the Church, to recognize that she was founded by Jesus on the rock of St. Peter. We hold tightly to our plans, our purses, our career choices, our messed-up friends and culture-saturated colleagues, our children, our timing for procreation, our efforts to appear youthful forever, and even our insanely fast-paced schedules.

Submission and humility are not part of our culture.

Beauty, degrees, bank accounts, and inflated pride—we cling to these things. We let them rule our lives.

If we humble ourselves in the sight of the Lord, life becomes sweet. Instead, we let life trample all over us, believing it can give us a few things we desperately want. When life fails to deliver on the joy it promised, only then are we ready to give God what's left.

I have embraced almost every lie our culture dangles before us. And I have the scars to prove it.

But the pain that came after the dust settled cannot be overstated. I remember the day the whole thing imploded. I was living in my parents' basement. My three half-grown children had just traveled from St. Louis to Atlanta to spend the summer with their dad. They called to say they had arrived safely, and my daughter announced that their stepmom was pregnant.

I sat on my bed and tried to keep my emotions in check until the phone call ended.

Nothing prepares a woman's heart for things like this. Nothing prepares her for the news that her children have a stepmother, that her husband has a new wife, that they will share the delight of bringing a child into this world, especially when the rejected one is living in her parents' basement and her children are visiting their father for six long weeks. Nothing prepares a woman for the realization that she deliberately and irrevocably ended her own chances of ever having another baby through sterilization, and yet the rest of her family will experience that joy with someone else.

I encountered humility through total humiliation—a result of my own life choices. The preacher's

kid and former preacher's wife was now the divorced
mother of three. I sat on my bed for a very long time and
felt the weight of so many mistakes.

Perhaps humiliation has been your introduction to
humility as well. Maybe you have been burdened down
by sin in the past, too.

Here's the amazing thing. Mother Church was
waiting for me. She was there to pick up the pieces and
see what needed to be healed. She was able to determine
what it all meant and why it all went wrong. I thought
the annulment process would be something like opening
Pandora's box. It turned out to be one of the most healing experiences of my life. Mother Church helped me
to begin again and live again in a rightly-ordered way.
The only thing that has come to me with more healing
power is the confessional and the Real Presence of Jesus
Christ in the Eucharist.

When my marriage to a minister fell apart and I
lost my pastor-father through death, I went to Mother
Church as one humiliated and humbled. And that was
the beginning of a new life, a new marriage, a new faith,
and even a new me.

I didn't enter the Church at Easter Vigil as so many
other adults have done. My resistance to fill out the
annulment papers delayed my entry by a few months.
But I learned some important lessons as I waited to
receive the Eucharist. Our Church is on our side. She
wants us whole and happy. And she knows that whole-
ness and happiness come through Christ. Today, I am
free to receive Jesus Christ in the Eucharist. I am able to
become a living tabernacle for the King of kings. And
when I fall, when I stumble and render myself unworthy,

I have access to the Sacrament of Reconciliation. God has made a way through the desert, through the back roads, through the hills. God has made a way through the death of a parent, through divorce and humiliations, through struggles and biases and preconceived notions. In the Gospel of Matthew, Jesus says, "Come to me, all you who labor and are burdened, and I will give you rest. Take my yoke upon you and learn from me, for I am meek and humble of heart; and you will find rest for your selves. For my yoke is easy, and my burden light" (Mt 11:28–30). And it is.

Mary and Elizabeth knew this to be true long before the first disciples heard our Lord speak of humble hearts. Indeed, even as the first whispers of the Gospel story echoed through the hills of Judea by way of Mary's feet, humility was leading the way. What pride had destroyed in the first garden, humility would rebuild. What arrogance had shattered, meekness would restore.

It is an invitation to us to walk in God's abundant life, to leave humiliations behind, to let them be purged in the confessional. Get out everything that stands between you and really living. You have been called to the freedom that comes in following Christ. Humility is beautiful. It is lovely.

Humility is a hand opening to God—a relaxing of the tightly squeezed fist that clings to all the false promises the world sets before us. Yes, humility is good. It is an open hand, a bent knee, a bowed head, a blessing poured out upon you. It's a finger that lifts your chin and says, "You are mine, and I have always loved you. Walk in the path I planned for you when I created you in the hidden place of your mother's womb."

Let the rest go. Travel lightly, like Mary. It is the only way to climb the hills that lie before us so that we can take Jesus to others. Imagine that you are like Mary, that there are some people living in those hills who will not know about the Lord if you do not go—because, really, that is very much the way of it.

But only the humble heart can travel these roads safely. Only the humble heart will recognize the Mother of God when she calls out. Yes, who are we that the Mother of our Lord should come to us? And yet, she has!

$\mathscr{R}$EFLECTION

What things do I cling to that stifle the spirit of humility? Am I confused about God's riches and blessings, considering them a result of my holiness or worthiness rather than the gifts of grace that they are? Am I ready to let go of my attachments to what the world promises and to embrace completely God's gifts in my life? How long has it been since I visited the confessional and lost the false me? Is it time for me to seek Christ in the Sacrament of Reconciliation and lose the extra baggage so that I can make this journey through the hills with Mary?

$\mathscr{L}$ord, give me a spirit of humility. Help me to empty myself of everything that might get in the way of serving you fully. I recognize that all that is good in my life is really a gift from you. Teach me

humility, through the witness of your mother and St. Elizabeth. Fill me now with the Holy Spirit so that I, like Mary, may be a living tabernacle. For your glory. Amen.

CHAPTER SIX

ᴀ Spirit of Adventure

Faith is a kind of journey whether we realize it or not.
Maybe your faith journey has been taking place on a
level just below your consciousness. It's like that for a lot
of Catholics. Each event in one's life within the Church
has been a kind of mile marker—Baptism, Confirmation,
marriage, raising children, the liturgical seasons, illness,
death of a parent, death of a spouse. The sacraments
have come to you at the right moment, bringing just the
right help for the journey.

This faith journey may have begun when you were
so young that you may not even remember those early
days of faith. Your parents carried you at first. They put

75

you on the path, taking you by the hand. You walked together like that, perhaps for many years. Then, your parents let you run ahead, entrusting you to the journey.

We're all on a spiritual journey whether we are aware of it or not. But there is a definite advantage to knowing that life is a faith journey, to embracing that journey with a kind of deliberateness as Mary did. We must follow our path as if it is the Jordan River, leading us to our own Ein Kerem and to those who are waiting for us to bring Christ to them. Too many Catholics sit down and take a rest after they are confirmed or once they head off to college. Sometimes, that hiatus lasts decades. Sometimes, it lasts their entire lives.

But our lives are part of the divine plan, and we are called to have a spirit of adventure as we journey toward heaven. This means we don't grow lazy or hide behind the walls of what is familiar or easy.

Like Mary, our job is to "Christify" the world. And we can't do that—we can't even encounter Christ, let alone share him—if we stay in the familiar "bedroom" of our "Nazareth" home. If we make it to Mass and leave it at that—or if we abandon the Eucharist completely—we will fail at our one, true job. We are called to carry Christ with us, holding him within our hearts after receiving him at Mass, and then sharing him with those we encounter beyond the church doors.

Theologian George Weigel reminds us that we have the ultimate responsibility of taking Christ "into all of those parts of 'the world' to which the laity has greater access than those who are ordained."[1] Our task is to share Jesus with others. We all have an Elizabeth in our lives—one who is ready and eager to receive Christ. We all have a Joseph in our lives—one who doesn't understand yet but, with a little grace, will embrace the truth so swiftly that we will be left breathless. We all have a Nazareth—those who do not understand, those who may become hostile if we share Christ with them, and yet Jesus Christ wants us to share even with them.

The mandate to share Christ reminds us of the words of St. John Paul II: "No believer in Christ, no institution of the Church can avoid this supreme duty: to proclaim Christ to all peoples."[2] We do not exist for ourselves. We exist to receive Christ and to bear Christ to the world, as Mary did. It's time to get up, get walking, and get back to the "Spring of the Vineyard"—our personal Ein Kerem. Even if the road takes you through some pretty rugged terrain rather than by the peaceful streams of the Jordan River, this journey is worth taking.

Once again, Mary is our model. She didn't sit around and wait for Christ to announce himself to the world. She thought about what Gabriel said and took to the road, going to the first place she was sure would receive the Good News with joy. Mary embodies the spiritual dynamic of the sending at the end of Mass. She listened to the Word of the Lord. She received Christ. She went out to proclaim Christ to those she knew best. Our Lord's Sacred Heart propelled Mary from Nazareth to the home of Zechariah and Elizabeth just as the Church sends us forth to share Christ with the world.

My first efforts to share my newly-found faith were a mixed bag. Sometimes, there is success right away when we share Christ. And sometimes, the success comes later. I experienced immediate results and also a lot of painful hits and misses.

A year after I converted, my youngest child entered the Church. That was easy. It was like journeying in the cooler months along the Jordan River. One day, my husband said it would be okay to put our daughter in our Parish School of Religion (PSR). He had one simple reason, and it had nothing to do with assent to the Catholic faith. In 1988, my husband graduated from a Catholic high school in St. Louis, Missouri. In St. Louis, the Catholic high schools are known for quality education. Many non-Catholics, like John's dad, place their children in Catholic schools simply because the parents know their sons and daughters will receive an excellent education. My husband remembered feeling like the odd duck as the only Protestant in a sea of Catholic boys attending St. John Vianney High School. If there was even a chance that our daughter would go to a Catholic high school, John wanted her to fit in. And so, when she was in first grade, he told me to call the parish and see what I needed to do so that she could enter the Church.

It was wonderful to have Jennifer with me at Mass. She took to the faith easily. I rejoiced, because my youngest child would never struggle with inherited biases against the faith. She would encounter the faith with as much ease as a cradle Catholic.

My husband's conversion was another story. Sharing the Catholic faith with him was more like journeying through the steeper hills in the hottest months of the year in order to arrive at Ein Kerem, rather than traveling leisurely along the Jordan Valley. Once Jennifer received her First Holy Communion, I longed for my husband to be beside us at Mass and to know the joy of Christ in the Eucharist. But his conversion seemed unlikely.

While John was raised Baptist, much of his extended family was Catholic. His parents' siblings had married Catholics and raised their children in the Catholic Church. But John's mom was Baptist, and John and his sister first discovered God's love through their mother in a Baptist church.

When John was in middle school, his mother died of breast cancer. He tried to go to church regularly for a while, but it just became too difficult without a mother's prompting. John's dad decided to send his son to a Catholic high school, hoping it would provide a solid social and academic setting for the boy who had experienced a terrible loss at such a tender age.

After high school, John headed off to college, but church wasn't a big part of this phase of his life. One day, while commuting to graduate school, he heard on the radio that the Oklahoma City Federal Building had been bombed. The tragic news made John take stock of his life, and he decided that it was time to return to his faith and stop ignoring God. Life is transitory and fleeting, and he saw the necessity of an immovable faith.

John and I met about a year later. The timing was ideal. I needed some ballast in my life. John was rock solid, and that was an important thing to a single mother of three young children. After a brief engagement, we married. We attended the Presbyterian church where my father was the pastor. When Dad became ill and left pastoral ministry, we attended the Baptist church where John's mother had taken him as a small boy. Then my father died, and I went searching for answers.

"I think I'm supposed to become Catholic," I told John one day. He said that was fine, but he wasn't interested in becoming Catholic. I agreed to keep my Catholic journey private. I thought that would be enough. In time, however, things changed. I began to know the faith well enough to share it, and I wanted everyone I loved to have access to Jesus Christ in the Eucharist. I especially wanted that for my husband.

But it doesn't always happen that others are ready to receive the Good News the moment you are ready to share it. My husband wasn't ready.

Grace has its own timetable. Mary understood that well. Another's free will can't be forced. We each know a before-the-dream Joseph—someone who has not experienced the necessary outpouring of grace that leads to understanding. Grace takes her own sweet time.

I wondered how some wives went decades like this, slogging through years of waiting. I prayed for my husband's conversion, but I admit, I didn't think it would ever happen.

I tried to argue my husband into the Church without success. Every time we talked about religion, we ended up in an argument. I knew God couldn't possibly have intended us to be at odds when he called me into the Church, but I didn't know what to do with this ache. I felt on fire to share the Good News of Christ in the Eucharist, but the one I loved most wanted to hear nothing about it. All of the safe ground—all of those topics that didn't go into faith and religion—they all seemed to be merely small talk to me now. We muddled through that time, steering our conversations to more peaceful topics, but those conversations seemed stale. It was like eating soda crackers on Thanksgiving. It's something, but heavens, it could be so much better.

I'd had enough of safe topics: how Jen's piano lessons went, what we needed from the grocery store, what came in the mail, who had left a voicemail. With simple questions, answers, comments, we kept it safe. If life is an adventure, I sure didn't expect the adventure to look like this.

"Remember St. Monica," my parish priest said. "Would she have become a saint if she had not had a son who needed her prayers? And then we never would have had St. Augustine." Okay, that's fair enough, I thought.

So, I prayed—and I stopped arguing with John.

On Christmas Eve 2007, John went to Mass with us, and he passed me a Christmas card before Mass began. I opened the card and read the words he had written inside—words that described how deeply he loves me and how that had prompted him to consider the Catholic Church. "And so, I join the Church this coming Easter." That was the final sentence. John told me that he had been secretly studying with our parish RCIA leader for months but had waited to tell me until he was sure that he would convert.

I thought back to the conversations I'd had recently with our RCIA leader—how he'd said it was a small class that year, just one guy, so they were doing private instruction together. That one guy was my husband!

God has an amazing spirit of adventure. He replaces discord with harmony. He makes all things new. But we must be willing to go through the discord, the tears, the trauma, the tragedy. To do that, we must have a powerful spirit of adventure.

The first person I told after Christmas Eve Mass was my friend Beth. She had joined me in petitioning Mary for this gift of grace—as Elizabeth must have prayed for Joseph when she and Mary shared their deepest longings with one another at the Visitation.

Soon, I was invited to be a guest on *The Journey Home* and *Women of Grace* to share the story of my conversion and talk about being a Catholic writer. Doors opened. The pace picked up. Every month God provided a new venue for writing.

My spiritual journey cut through some densely populated areas. During this time, Beth's journey moved to higher ground—far from the public eye—where views were gorgeous, but the journey was not for the faint of heart. We marveled because whether the journey went deeper into the crowds or deeper into the quiet, the double garment of Mary and Jesus was ours.

Many people prefer the fast-paced journey in which the crowds gather rather than the steep inclines that provide majestic views coupled with great spiritual endurance. But when I consider both paths, I realize something. The safer path is the harder path—the one Beth has chosen.

I continue to do what God has placed before me, but I do so by holding tightly to my friend's hand. There will come a day when God will lead others down this fast-paced lane to share God's Good News with the crowds, and he will whisper to me that it is time to walk a path similar to Beth's. In that moment, I will let her help pull me up the incline. I will remember her words:

"Let it go. We must not cling to the road. We cling to Mary and Jesus."

I wonder if that's how it was for Mary after Jesus ascended into heaven. We know Mary was busy. So many souls needed to be mothered. So many needed the Church to lead them to Christ in the Eucharist. The Holy Spirit poured forth upon the people, and Mary must have recognized that she had much to do. And then, her Son called to her. She was asked to pursue a steeper path, a higher vision, with majestic views, where she would be able to accomplish far more. Raised to realms on high, she would reign with her Son, where she would be able to intercede for all—guiding disciples along their busy paths, and picking up sinners and pointing them in the right direction.

This Mother has always had a spirit of adventure. And she teaches us to have that same spirit. She whispers to us: *What is the Father asking of you?*

Mary shows us how to travel along the Jordan River, through the valley where so many gather. She also leads us up, through the Judean hills, where the path is not so easy to follow, but where the winds of the Holy Spirit blow powerfully and angels keep one's feet from dashing against the stones.

What adventure lies before you? Are there aspects to that adventure that scare you? Do you sense that it's time to change jobs, make new friends, start attending daily Mass? Is there someone who has a special mission that resonates with you, that awakens a desire in you to serve in a similar way? Do you get the feeling that the hills are calling you to come and explore them? Are you afraid you aren't up to the challenge, fearing that you aren't fit for it, spiritually or physically? And yet, is something nudging you forward?

Jesus calls us to this Gospel adventure—just as he called his own Mother when he was still in her womb. Once we have Christ within us, we become his disciples. And disciples are not meant to gain knowledge and become anointed followers only to sit around and do nothing. Disciples must learn from that first and best disciple of Christ. We must learn from Mary. She listened to the Word, received Christ, and went out to proclaim him.

She left her comfort zone, and God invites you to do the same. She journeyed down every path God laid before her, and God invites you to do the same. Though she was a meek and humble Jewish girl, content to live a life of quiet fidelity to God, she embraced every spiritual adventure. If she could take to the roads and answer the Spirit's call to adventure with purpose and zeal, then we can as well. For this, we were created.

ℛEFLECTION

What adventure is waiting for me? Does my love for Christ in the Eucharist continue to burn within me when I enter the work week? Are my hands ready and my tongue quick to share Christ when another seems receptive? Would I share Christ even with those who are not receptive, knowing that God wants to reach everyone? Am I willing to become a contemplative, a quiet intercessor, if my call is changing and God wants me to follow him to higher ground? How can I leave my comfort zone today and open myself up to the adventure God has in mind for me?

Lord, give me a spirit of adventure. Help me to choose the path that you have set before me. Give me a sense of purpose and zeal for souls that is so clearly present in Mary's life. Reveal your plan for me as I study your mother's life and seek to follow her lead in sharing you with others. For your glory. Amen.

CHAPTER SEVEN

A Spirit of Hospitality

I do not have a natural inclination toward hospitality. In fact, I could easily become a reclusive writer, with my slight tendencies toward agoraphobia. I am most comfortable in my own home. When phone calls come in, I prefer to screen them, and I'd rather have my husband field visits by the repairman while I hide out with our labradoodle, Max, in the back bedroom.

Not only do I not possess hospitality on a natural level, but I have to pray to have even the desire for a spirit of hospitality. That's problematic because a spirit of hospitality is essential in the work of sharing Christ with the world. Without hospitality, we do more harm than good. I know this to be true just as I know holiness requires visits to the confessional and frequent reception of Jesus Christ in the Holy Eucharist. I know it as I know that conversion isn't possible without grace. I know it because I know that hospitality is love in action. A spirit of hospitality is an essential gift for those who wish to share Jesus Christ with others.

But for me, the gift of hospitality is a supernatural gift; it is not a gift I have received on the natural order. It is not part of my DNA at all. I share this with you so that you will be encouraged. You don't have to have a natural affinity for each gift listed in these chapters. Supernatural help is available when your DNA is insufficient.

The spirit of hospitality in the Gospel story is most palpable in the moment Mary steps across the threshold of Zechariah and Elizabeth's home. Mary left the safety and comfort of her home in order to share Christ with Elizabeth, Zechariah, and a yet-unborn John the Baptist. That is hospitality. Elizabeth also displays a spirit of hospitality by receiving Mary with superabundant joy and charity.

But there's something more profound going on here.

According to Cardinal Carlo Maria Martini, this encounter is not only a matter of Mary visiting Elizabeth or Elizabeth receiving Mary; it is (according to biblical language and Hebrew tradition) a visitation from God.[1] It seems odd to think of God as acting with a spirit of hospitality, but that is precisely what he does at the Visitation. God visits and God receives—visiting and receiving both Mary and Elizabeth. Furthermore, God visits and receives a yet-unborn John, who leaps while within the womb at the sound of Mary's voice. This "anointing" of John is the first example of God's desire to work through Mary, not only to bring about the Incarnation, but also to use her as a coworker in his great plan of redemption. God moves through her.

And God desires to work through us, to move through us, to enlist our help as coworkers in his great plan.

In the first chapter of St. Luke's Gospel, Our Lady of Grace is already being used to bring God's favor and anointing to those she encounters: to Elizabeth, to the unborn John, to Zechariah. God visits the house of Zechariah, and he does it by way of Mary. These encounters hearken back to the divine visitation that occurred between Abraham and God's messengers, which in turn reminds the reader of the encounter between Moses and God. Quite literally, God is with these two women. He is truly in their presence and remains with them, in the second person of the Blessed Trinity.

By the time Mary arrives at Elizabeth's home, Mary has said yes to a number of spiritual gifts. She has displayed a spirit of spontaneity in her response to Archangel Gabriel. She has shown great courage in welcoming the Son of God into her womb. She has permitted joy to become her strength, to make her ready for anything. Her humility undergirded every decision and marked each quiet moment of contemplation. She embraced God's great, unfolding adventure. And now, the fulfillment of the Visitation is finally actualized through the gift of hospitality. This is the gift that takes on flesh. It manifests itself through hands and feet and action. It is

more verb than noun, more doing than being. It is faith
with works.

As always, the one who receives Christ is expected
to share Christ. When that happens, God visits the
world. When that happens, God receives the world to
himself. And it becomes a moment of divine hospitality. The preeminent divine visitation and manifestation
of hospitality occurred at Ein Kerem when Mary was
received by Elizabeth.

As an evangelical Protestant, I often found Catholic
terms unfamiliar. But the word *visitation* should not be
considered foreign to the Christian tongue. What other
word could be more fitting than this word—*Visitation*—
to describe Christ's coming to Elizabeth and his remaining with her throughout Mary's three-month visit?

Is this visit a quiet vignette added to the biblical
text solely to advance the narrative? No. This Visitation
has been in the mind of God for a long time. This journey to the hill country has a precedent. We have seen
this before. Old Testament scholars are quick to point
to 1 Samuel 6 as the prefiguration of Mary's visit to
Elizabeth's home. In this passage of Sacred Scripture,
David exclaims, "How can the ark of the Lord come to
me?" David leaves the Ark in the hill country of Judea
for three months. He dances and leaps before the Ark,
just as John leaps in the womb of his mother when she
encounters Mary.

Mary is the Ark of a New Covenant. Within her
womb, she carries the fulfillment of the Law and the
Bread of Life. And she visits Elizabeth to share the ultimate gift of God's Son.

Mary becomes the first one to share Jesus Christ with another human being. Every divine visitation that came before the Annunciation and Visitation foreshadowed these events. Every divine visitation that has occurred since then circles back to those events. In the first chapter of St. Luke's gospel, we see a display of divine love that will expand to encompass people of every time, every tongue, and every nation.

This display of divine love needs our cooperation. Like Mary, we are being called to become a conduit for a divine visitation. We are called to participate in divine hospitality.

And what about Elizabeth's role in the Visitation? Elizabeth's reception and reaction provide a fuller perspective on the dawning of the Gospel story.

How did Elizabeth receive this sudden visit by Mary? Today, we would have had ample notice before a visitor dropped in. Mary would have had a cell phone. She would have called or texted to say she was on her way. The two women might have planned a visit before Mary hopped in her car and told a built-in phone app to get directions to Ein Kerem. Almost instantly, the smartphone would begin spewing forth directions.

But this visit was unexpected. If Elizabeth had any inkling that Mary was about to drop in for a visit, it's because life already had a serendipitous feel to it, and Elizabeth had learned to roll quickly with divine surprises. Elizabeth and Zechariah had been blessed with a most unusual pregnancy. Maybe they were already expecting their days to contain one unusual event after another.

Sure, they were old, like Sarah and Abraham. Sure, an angel had announced the pregnancy to Zechariah. Yes, Elizabeth and Zechariah were part of the greater salvation story. But something was different with this birth announcement. God's message to Zechariah at the Temple indicated that the fullness of time was at hand. The Messiah's arrival was not some distant event on the horizon. Their Messiah was coming soon! It wouldn't be a few more centuries, or after a couple of generations, or even in a few decades. God had said Elizabeth and Zechariah's son would announce the arrival of the Messiah. That could only mean that the time of the Lord's coming was upon them.

Soon, God would visit them in one magnificent display of divine hospitality. Behold, your Messiah has come!

Elizabeth knew these things. She must have daydreamed now and then about who the Messiah's mother would be and how Elizabeth's own son would meet the One. For Elizabeth and Zechariah, that era of their marriage must have been surreal.

Elizabeth merits study for many reasons, but for one reason in particular. In welcoming Mary into her home, Elizabeth welcomes Christ into her home. Elizabeth is the first person in all of human history to invite the Sacred Heart of Jesus to take up residence within her home! She is a true participant in divine hospitality. For all those Catholics who have a special space in their home for the enthronement of the Sacred Heart, you share a special kinship with Elizabeth. Like her, you are participating in a divine visitation, a kind of divine hospitality. You have said, "God is welcome here in my home."

It is difficult to imagine what was going through Elizabeth's mind when Mary showed up on her doorstep, or when a yet-unborn John leaped in her womb, or when the Holy Spirit announced in the recesses of Elizabeth's heart, "This is the Mother, and you are standing in the presence of God!" What must that have been like for Elizabeth?

Even with all of the mystery, even with all of her own joy, she was not so lost in the daydreaming that she could not properly welcome the Lord and his mother into her home. Elizabeth knew what to do. Mary called out, and *Elizabeth went to her* with the greatest joy and welcomed her relative into her home. The spirit of welcome and the spirit of true hospitality were not forgotten in the divinely-inspired meeting.

I have no delusions about how I would have responded. I would have been so wrapped up in my own amazing call that I might have seen only a distant relative who dropped in without advance notice. My slight agoraphobia may have brought uncharitable thoughts to mind. *Couldn't my cousin have visited before all of the excitement began? I don't think I have time for this right now. Yes, it is good to see her, but really, now? Zechariah is mute. I'm pregnant. I'm not nearly as young as she is! And now she becomes my guest! I'm barely able to keep the house clean and the meals on the table for Zechariah and me. I fall into bed at night with aches in places where I have never ached before. And suddenly, a teenager decides to move in. How long did you say you are planning to stay, Mary? Until my baby comes? So much for privacy.*

But that is not Elizabeth at all. Instead, Elizabeth praises God. Such generosity is hard to imagine. She immediately moves from inward focus to outward focus and proclaims, "Most blessed are *you* among women, and blessed is the fruit of *your* womb. And how does this happen to me, that the mother of my Lord should come to me? For at the moment the sound of your greeting reached my ears, the infant in my womb leaped for joy. Blessed are you who believed that what was spoken to you by the Lord would be fulfilled" (Lk 1:42–45).

Elizabeth rejoices with Mary. She thanks God for the coming Messiah *and* for the holy woman that will bear the Son of God. She recognizes her own smallness and her own unmerited favor that Mary should come to her home.

Elizabeth models for us the perfect response to God's visitation: to be people full of joy and gratitude, ready with open homes and open hearts and open lives. Moreover, Elizabeth was willing to give the gift she carried within her for the glory of God that the world would know that *the Messiah has come.*

While we know these things hinted at the miraculous aspect of their pregnancies, let's pause to consider and learn from the practical side of things. The Visitation is marked by the spirit of hospitality, and hospitality always stems from a desire to serve in very practical ways. These two women know how to serve one another, for love of God. And because God loved them, he brought them together so that they might assist one another in fulfilling their unique missions.

God knew that Mary would need some preparation for the birth of his Son. He knew she would be alone—except for Joseph—when the Messiah arrived. There would be no midwife. Mary's own mother would not be there.

God brought these two women together for very practical reasons. Mary learned firsthand what to expect during the final months of pregnancy and what to do when she gave birth. There really is no doubt that they talked about practical aspects of childbearing. Every woman who has ever given birth has turned to another woman, a trusted woman, and peppered her with questions.

Mary was not the only one who required practical assistance. One can assume that Mary became Elizabeth's greatest champion, a necessary help for an elderly woman about to bear a child late in life. Imagine how Elizabeth's pregnancy affected her: aching back, aching feet, sciatic-nerve issues, preeclampsia, gestational diabetes. How did Elizabeth cope with third-trimester pregnancy? Did Elizabeth ache from the moment her feet hit the ground in the morning? Perhaps Mary rubbed Elizabeth's feet or massaged her weary back. No doubt, she helped with household chores and urged Elizabeth to rest whenever possible. Even on a strictly practical level, Elizabeth would have thought that Mary was a gift from God.

Christ asks us to learn from Mary. We are to meet the temporal needs of others, always with hope that it will bear fruit for the kingdom of God. We are to receive others as though receiving Christ himself. The spirit of hospitality is a spirit of giving and receiving, a spirit of release, and a spirit of welcome. Mary and Elizabeth embodied this spirit perfectly.

Is it time to take a look around you and see who needs some practical assistance? Who needs a little help just to get through the day? Can you become Mary to another Elizabeth? Perhaps you have overlooked someone because you tend to see things from your own perspective and are caught in the trap of elevating yourself and your own position as a Christ-bearer. Is there someone who is not seen by the crowds, but who is far greater than you in this mission to share Christ? Can you receive that one with hospitality even as Elizabeth received Mary into her home?

If hospitality is not a gift you possess on a natural level, are you open to receiving some supernatural help in this area?

I do not have a servant's heart by nature. I rely heavily on a supernatural deposit of grace to bestow upon me what I need in order to serve others. Yes, I am ashamed to admit it, but my heart for service comes to me by grace and not through DNA. But God has come to me in my weakness, and he has made me strong.

One example of divine intervention took place in February 2011. It seemed as if I was in over my head. My middle daughter was moving back home—with her two infant sons. The long-term relationship with her boyfriend was over.

I was both happy and immensely concerned. Did I have what it takes to lay down my life for my grown daughter and her little boys? I had never been the most patient mother. Would I drive my daughter further away while she lived with us? Would my lack of patience and fear of being taken advantage of ruin whatever grace God wanted to bring to the lives of these three people?

This was an opportunity to be Christ to them—but was I strong enough for the job?

The guest room became a little apartment. The crib was up. The play-and-pack was ready. We moved an empty dresser into the room and bought a toddler bed, diapers, and a few toys. Everything was ready—except me.

On the Friday before their arrival, I made a special trip to a nearby parish to meet with Fr. Timothy Elliott. In the confessional, I laid out the situation. I told him honestly how ill-equipped I was for this life event. I confided in him that I longed to see my daughter convert, but I also knew that I was far more likely to drive her away than draw her in.

Fr. Elliott listened. He nodded as I talked. And then he asked me if I had a pocket crucifix. I told him that I did not. He recommended that I buy one. "Carry it in your pocket. When you feel you don't have enough strength to be a witness with your words or actions, reach into your pocket and hold on tight. He will give you what you need."

My husband found a pocket-sized St. Benedict crucifix and bought it for me. Kari moved home with her two little boys and a standard poodle. Suddenly, used bottles and dirty clothes were everywhere. A baby was always crying and needed to be held and loved and read to and fed.

I returned to the field of teaching to mitigate the extra financial burden and get our own personal finances in better shape. God blessed me with an amazing group of students, but the work was exhausting, and it seemed

we had one family crisis after another during that time.
I felt torn in many directions.

Sometimes, we barely held on to our sanity. Sometimes, tempers flared. But always, there was grace.

By this time, God had planted a wonderful priest in
our local parish, and Fr. Tom Miller became my spiritual
director. He kept me grounded in the faith and enabled
me to practice levels of service to my family that I never
thought possible.

There were times when we were able to share the
faith with Kari, but mostly, we shared Christ by our
actions. When we were successful, there was grace.
When we failed miserably, there was grace.

Eventually, Kari moved into her own apartment
a few miles away, and life took on a new rhythm. We
were still their second home and a source for laundry
facilities, but I had learned to hold on to Christ crucified
in all things.

Then, Kari announced that she was pregnant again.

This time, things were different. This time, she was
broken and ready. That third baby propelled her to the
Church in ways no words from me ever could. Within
a few months, every one of my grandsons was baptized
and my daughter had received Jesus Christ in the Eucharist. Her conversion made my husband's conversion
look like a walk in the park.

We had spent ourselves fully, and Jesus Christ
entered into every practical assistance and act of love
we could muster. My daughter was Catholic. Her new
son, little Levi, is the first cradle Catholic in our family!
We take up a row at Mass: John, me, two daughters, and

three grandsons. Less than ten years ago, not one of us was Catholic. God had visited us.

And he longs to visit you and your family members. He wants to enter your world and touch the people you touch. He wants to go to them by way of your feet, by the work of your hands. He wants to give you every gift you need whether through the natural deposit that is part of your DNA or through moments of grace that mold you into a person you never thought you could be. God wants to visit you.

God invites us to learn from Mary. We, too, are called to pour ourselves out for one another—even if we don't like to answer phones; even if we cringe when there is a knock at the door; even if we would rather be the anonymous Mass attender than join a group at church; and even if we are antisocial, lazy, or just incredibly busy. We are the hands and feet of Christ and we can carry him to others just as Mary once carried him to Ein Kerem on the power of her own two feet. We, too, can become a conduit for grace. Through us, God is able to visit the world today.

ℛEFLECTION

How do I respond when God makes a surprise visit to me? With joy? With gratitude? Do I throw open the doors even when it means altered plans? Do I serve the Lord in practical ways? Do I share Christ with others in what I do and not merely in what I say? Do I receive others as though receiving Christ himself? Do I have a pocket crucifix to hold when I feel weak or another devotional practice that helps me to practice the gift of hospitality? Which gifts are part of my natural DNA, and which gifts require an extra portion of divine assistance? Do I realize that all of these gifts, whether naturally given or supernaturally given, are truly gifts from God?

Lord, give me a spirit of hospitality. Help me to see the temporal needs of others and to generously meet those needs in whatever way I can. Give me a servant's heart, a willingness to serve that was so clearly present in Mary's life. Help me to remember that you visit others by way of my feet and by the work of my hands. For your glory. Amen.

CHAPTER EIGHT

A Spirit of Wonder and Awe

"The source of all sacred mystery is Christ among us, our hope of glory," declares St. Paul in his letter to the Colossians (1:28). The Visitation is a manifestation of this sacred mystery and glorious hope. At the Visitation, Elizabeth discovers something that we also are called to discover, something I did not realize for forty years.

It is the mystery and glorious hope of Christ living in Mary. Sacred Scripture establishes it, and the Church in time has experienced it. Mary magnifies Christ.

And if that is true—and it is—then this one who magnifies Christ also magnifies the mystery; the power; the glory; and the immutable, unshakable, and indestructible hope we encounter in Christ. For this reason, there is no danger in turning to Mary in order to see Christ, for it is in that moment that the Lord is magnified—not minimized—and our humanity bows low to honor Mary and to adore Christ.

In that moment, the gift of wonder and awe rises in our souls.

When we, like Elizabeth, utter the words, "Who am I that the Mother of my Lord should come to me?" it becomes the moment of our own visitation. In this moment we receive the double garment of which St. Louis de Montfort speaks—Jesus living in Mary, the glory of God reaching into our humanity, Immaculate Heart and Sacred Heart beating in unison. And we pause to enter the mystery.

During the chapter on the gift of courage, we were reminded that courage has been ours from the moment of our Confirmation. Wonder and awe, like courage, is a gift from the Holy Spirit, a gift given to us from the moment the bishop anointed us with chrism oil and said the words, "Be sealed with the Holy Spirit."

When we encounter divine mystery, the gift of wonder and awe rises within us and our heart responds. It is the "amen" of the soul. And yes, it is a gift from the Holy Spirit given to us from the moment of our Confirmation.

I remember the day I discovered the joy of playing with a prism and realized the power contained in a magnifying glass. I was sitting on the windowsill of our fifth-grade classroom and chatting with friends. We

were looking at Mrs. Grace's plants and goofing around
with the magnifying glasses and prisms. I was capti-
vated by the rainbows appearing on our notebook paper
when we held a prism "just so" between our fingers and
thumb. What an amazing thing, this ray of sunlight! I
studied the spectrum, trying to figure out just where one
color ended and another began.

My friend Maridee was playing with the magnifying glass. She was fascinated by the pinpoint of bright
light that she could generate by steadily holding the
magnifying glass in one position and letting the sunlight pass through the glass. There were other students
there, too, but I remember Maridee vividly, sitting by the
window. As we watched and laughed at the wonders
of science, her paper began to smoke, and the little spot
of bright light turned brown where the magnified rays
scorched the paper. And then, the flame became visible
and began to consume the paper! Nobody said a word,
but we all sucked in our breath in one collective gasp.

Some may choose to look at Christ through prisms,
longing only to see rainbows and sunshine, but the ultimate power and glory are made manifest when he is
magnified, when his creation offers itself up as an obla-
tion—a burnt offering that has encountered the con-
suming fire of God. We are stunned, rendered silent,
like children holding burning paper in one hand and
the magnifying glass in the other hand.

Here, there is power and glory. Here, we see the
mystery of Christ among us. And here, we respond with
wonder and awe.

Elizabeth was the first to recognize Christ living in
Mary. In fact, more than thirty years before Peter hails

Jesus as "the Messiah, the Son of the living God" (Mt
16:16), long before the crowds proclaim, "Blessed is she
who bore you and fed you from her breasts" (see Lk
11:27), Elizabeth understands and bows low in wonder and awe. We must do the same. These two women
rejoiced in the great mystery that Christ was *among*
them, and for Mary specifically, the mystery was Christ
living *within* her.

How can we appreciate the weight of that secret—
what Mary held within her womb as she traveled? How
can we fathom what it was like to climb those hills as she
journeyed to Ein Kerem, as she stood on one mountain-
top after another and felt the cool wind rushing full in
her face? How can we begin to understand what Mary
knew?

I think of the day I climbed the hill to the Church of
the Visitation in Ein Kerem. Red-faced and thoroughly
exhausted, I made that final ascent, stood before the
church, and let my eyes follow the steeple into the heavens. What was it like for Mary to stand at the apex of that
hill—and of every Judean hill that came before it—and
let her eyes lay claim to the land and to the whole world,
in the name of her Son? What was it like to know that,
in just a few minutes, she would see Elizabeth? And the
words Mary kept within her would have ears ready to
hear and a soul ready to praise God with her. Soon, there
would be another person who would marvel with her
at the awesome work their God had done.

This child was Israel's hope. This was the Lion of
Judah, the Desire of Nations, Messiah, Mighty One,
Prince of Peace, the Sun of Righteousness. The names
of Old Testament prophecy echoed through the hills

as Mary made her way to Elizabeth's home, for within Mary's womb, she carried the Holy One of Israel.

Mary must have realized that just a glimpse of a pregnant Elizabeth would underscore something more—something greater—something Israel yearned to see. It would point to everything the angel had said: "For nothing will be impossible for God."

The Messiah had come to a virgin as promised by the prophets, as announced by the angel. And the *forerunner* of that Messiah was alive and kicking in the expanding womb of an old woman. Elizabeth's baby was the first visible sign that God was fulfilling his promise to Israel.

Mary headed for the hills of Judea, in part, because she longed to be with the only person on earth who could possibly understand this great, holy mystery. Mary was not looking for proof; she did not doubt what the angel had said. But somehow, being with Elizabeth would be like hearing those divine words over, and over, and over. *Nothing is impossible with God. Nothing is impossible with God.* And together, the gift of wonder and awe would rise up. The "amen" of the soul, the gift that comes as a response to divine mystery, would come forth.

The fleeting encounter with Archangel Gabriel remained with Mary in a tangible way through the visible reality of Elizabeth's third-trimester pregnancy. Elizabeth's body would bear witness to something Mary already knew: the angel had gotten everything right.

It was the most incredible if/then scenario. If God could make an old woman who had never been fertile *be fertile*, then a virgin could conceive. If the final prophet

was about to be born, then the Messiah's birth was also
imminent. If Elizabeth . . . then Mary. If John the Baptist
. . . then Jesus Christ! God had entered their humanity,
and nothing would be the same.

What was it like for Elizabeth to miss that first
period? Or was she far beyond the years of monthly
cycles and therefore oblivious to the first weeks of the
baby's gestation? What was it like for her to experience the first signs of morning sickness? To find herself
loosening the tie at her waist because her middle was
expanding, and it wasn't because she was experiencing
a midlife weight gain? What was it like to anticipate her
son's first kick? To know it would all happen—baby
kicks and lactating breasts—all of it? She was having a
baby! What a miraculous, incredible, almost zany life
she and Zechariah had been given! And to think she
could not even talk it out with her husband—for Zechariah was unable to speak. But now, Mary had come.
Now, the Messiah's mother was experiencing all of this
with Elizabeth.

One can barely grasp the profound mystery that
knit these two women together. Though Elizabeth has
conceived the prophet and not the Messiah, she, too,
bears the mark of divine mystery. It permits her to recognize the holy Mother of God at first glance! Think
about it—Elizabeth prefigures her son's role. She recognizes who Jesus is before anyone else, and she proclaims it. Just as Mary is the Mother of God, Elizabeth
is the mother of his prophet—and the Visitation reveals
something of the mystery connecting these two unborn
babies. The rest of the world saw only a young woman,
betrothed to a man from Nazareth. Elizabeth sees

beyond. She knows that the Old Covenant is giving way to the New Covenant. She embodies the old even as she receives the new. And in the moment Elizabeth receives Christ within Mary, Elizabeth is consumed, as if by fire, and filled with a spirit of wonder and awe, proclaiming, "The Mother of my Lord has come to me!"

In that moment, Elizabeth encounters the Lord's magnifier. And Elizabeth's soul is set ablaze.

The God who parted the waters for Israel, the God who swept away kingdoms and established Israel in their place, the God who made a donkey speak and a fish to spit a man upon dry land, the God who gave them food in the desert and water from a rock, the God who made the sun reverse its course and floods to cover the land, the God who saved men from lions and a fiery furnace, the God who wrote prophecy on a wall with his own hand—this God was doing his greatest work right here, in Mary's womb.

In fact, everything that came before them *pointed* to this moment. And Elizabeth understood. "Who am I that the Mother of my Lord—this amazing, awesome Lord of all creation and source of our salvation—should come to me?"

I can hear them laughing: Mary and Elizabeth— laughing and laughing. And then, I see them sitting quietly together, because words and laughter could never be enough to contain the mystery.

Sometimes, they must have simply sat together in the quiet—their babies moving and growing and waiting. After the quiet settled around them and their faces reflected the wonder of God, their eyes must have filled with tears of joy, and they probably quickly wiped them

away and went back to the very practical work of preparing a meal or clearing away the dishes. Words, laughter, silence, tears, and work—for three months, that was
the rhythm of life for these two women.

The spirit of wonder and awe dwells here. It is present in moments like this, moments when the rhythm of
our humanity invites the divine mystery to dwell with
us. It's present in moments when we invite Christ to join
us as we drive to work, or to the church for a once-in-
a-lifetime sacrament. It's present in moments when we
pick up groceries and buy flowers for our wives, or for
a parent's grave, or for the Mary garden. It's present in
moments when a grandchild spends the night, or we
visit an aging relative who once meant everything to
us. It's present in moments when we take our grief to
the adoration chapel, or perhaps we take the grief of
another there and intercede. It's present in moments
when we receive the Eucharist and deliberately set aside
the random thoughts in order to clear our head as we
receive him, or we deliberately take the more serious
life events to the Lord as we receive him. The spirit of
wonder and awe is where God visits us and where our
humanity embraces God.

We believe in signs and wonders and mystery
because we not only believe in the mystery of the Incarnation, but we believe in the mystery of the Holy Eucharist: Christ among us, our hope of glory. It's the verse I
cited at the beginning of this chapter. For Mary, for us,
the glorious reality is *Christ among us*—divinity entering
our humanity. And wonder and awe rise up.

It's like being in Mrs. Grace's room, Maridee holding the smoldering paper, and sitting together with her in silent wonder.

Mary and Elizabeth were content to live lives of quiet obscurity. They walked humbly with their God. They knew he had worked miracles in the past, and he would work miracles again, but they did not demand signs in order to believe. They served out of love. They were called to holiness, lowliness, and obedience in obscurity.

And then, God raised them to unimaginable heights and placed them at the nexus of *old* and *new*. Elizabeth's son is promised in the final verses of the Old Testament. He is the new Elijah. Mary's Son is promised throughout the Old Testament. He is the New Adam. When Elizabeth and Mary meet at the Visitation and throw their arms around one another, Old Covenant embraces New Covenant! Their embrace is a *tangible manifestation* of a spiritual reality. Something old is laying claim to something new. Something new is reaching out to something old. And at the center, we see Mary and Elizabeth.

But does God still enter into the human condition and fill us with wonder and awe? Yes, the mystery of God is all around us though we often dismiss it. In our own little lives and in countless ways, God inserts himself into our world.

If we pause to recognize the visitation, we open the door to the gift of wonder and awe. If we keep moving and choose to dismiss the mystery, we close the door on the gift.

In February, 1978, I was in eighth grade. From the very first waking moment, it felt odd to be getting dressed for school. The day seemed like a holiday or a snow day. A quick glance out the window nixed that possibility. I told my sister while we were making the bed, "It feels like we aren't going to have school today."

She laughed and said, "I wish."

A few minutes later I said it again. "It just feels like we aren't going to school, like we decided to get dressed for no reason."

About half an hour later, our neighbor saw us standing at our front window and stopped his truck. He motioned for us to come outside. I ran down the driveway to see what he wanted. He rolled his window down and said, "There isn't school today. Didn't you hear? They had a fire in the high school locker rooms last night. School's cancelled today."

My sister looked at me in disbelief. I knew what she was thinking. How could I have known?

Dad pulled me aside and asked me if anything like that had ever happened before. It had, once, when I was much younger. Dad told me that things like that happened to him occasionally, such as the day his little brother was almost killed in an accident while cutting trees on the family farm near Hillsboro, Wisconsin, or in the weeks that preceded my maternal grandfather's tragic death in a farming accident in northern Iowa.

As Dad spoke, I thought of a vision I'd had when I was nine—something I had never mentioned to anyone. I didn't even have a vocabulary to explain it when I was a child.

I remember being alone in the backyard. The church my dad pastored was behind me to my right, and the house we lived in was behind me to my left. I'd been thinking about the people who gave testimonies in church, how they praised God for rescuing them from a life of all sorts of vices and evils, and how God had turned their lives around. Just as quickly, I had the fleeting thought: "I wish that I could have a testimony that would inspire someone to love Jesus more." Instantly, I was sad because I believed that would never happen. I was a preacher's kid, "born again" by the age of eight, raised to know right from wrong. My life would not go badly enough to be an interesting story. These were the innocent thoughts of a Protestant preacher's daughter who had no idea that the world could be a toxic place. I thought I was saved—story over.

Then, suddenly, I saw myself as a middle-aged woman, seated in a room full of people. The people who filled that room had heard bits and pieces of my life, and they had come to hear the whole conversion story. I knew the woman I saw in the vision was me—an older me—but still me. And I knew, too, that what I saw was real.

I knew it, like I knew the double portion of the Spirit would fall to me after my father's death. I knew it, like I knew I had heard from Mary when a letter arrived on December 8, 2004. I knew it, like I knew that Jesus Christ is really present—body, blood, soul, and divinity—in the Most Blessed Sacrament. Somehow, all these things were tied together—because the Eucharist had been calling me to himself, and all these events pointed to him. The story I had to tell was *his story.*

You have seen this mystery play out in your own life. Every event has pointed to him. Your story is intertwined with the Eucharist. He has been calling you to

himself for as long as you can remember. It is a mystery
you do not fully grasp, but it is real. The mystery is
Christ in us—our hope of glory. Christ *is mystery*.

This mystery is as real as Mary stepping across the
threshold of Elizabeth's home. Jesus Christ has come to
us. And now, he enjoins us to share him with the world.
We have been entrusted with the totality of Christ's
message. Old Covenant, New Covenant; Church history from Abraham to Mary to Mother Teresa—Christ's
message must be shared. Talk about it. Laugh over it.
Sit in silence and contemplate it. Weep for joy because
of it. And get back to the work because of it. Like Mary
and Elizabeth once talked, laughed, sat in silence,
contemplated, wept, and worked in the hills of Judea
before anyone else in the world had preached the Good
News—so must we approach the mystery of God's presence with wonder and awe.

Then, we must do it all over again tomorrow—and
the next day, and the next. A spirit of wonder and awe
must infuse us with holy zeal. It must make our feet
restless enough to hit the road, journey near the Jordan,
climb the hills. The Good News must consume us until
we have to bear Christ to the world.

ℛEFLECTION

Where have I experienced the gift of wonder and awe
in the past? Do I make a habit of opening the door to
the divine mystery that ushers in this gift? Do I look
for Christ's presence in the day-to-day moments of my
life? Do I only look for him at Mass? Or do I look for

him to show up on a Tuesday morning when I'm driving to work? On a Friday night when I'm going out for dinner with my spouse? On a Saturday afternoon when I'm getting groceries? When I'm leaving on a business trip—or about to leave on a family vacation? What time of the day do I set aside to be with God, away from my busy life, for moments of contemplation, where God promises to show up?

Lord, help me to recognize your presence and to open myself up to the gifts I received at my Confirmation, especially the gift of wonder and awe. Remind me that Jesus Christ is the source of divine mystery, and that the easiest way to enter into that mystery is to sit at Mary's feet and learn from the one within whom the Word was made flesh. Give me a spirit of wonder and awe like that of Mary and Elizabeth. For your glory. Amen.

CHAPTER NINE

A Spirit of Thanksgiving

On Christmas Eve, 1985, the first pain hit at 9:30 p.m. I knew immediately that I had skipped early labor and entered active labor. At the hospital, the nurse called it "precipitate delivery." There would be no time for pain medicine. I was a little concerned about not receiving pain relief, but at least something was happening. I wouldn't be pregnant forever.

I looked at the clock and wondered if our baby would be born on Christmas Eve or Christmas Day. Then the nurse checked the heartbeat and the questions

about pain medicine and possible arrival time turned
into terrible silence. Something was wrong. The nurse
wasn't smiling. She just kept moving the obstetrical
stethoscope from one spot to another.

"I'm having trouble finding the heartbeat," she
said. After a few more attempts, she muttered something about getting the doctor, and I was left alone in the
small examination room. The wait was excruciating. I
knew what labor was like. I'd been through it two years
earlier. I couldn't imagine giving birth while overcome
by grief. Then, the doctor entered the room and found
the heartbeat. On Christmas Eve 1985, my son was born
just seven minutes before midnight. The wait was over.

Sometimes, waiting is like a game—fun, exciting.
Sometimes, waiting is a chore—demanding, requir-
ing effort. Sometimes, waiting is agonizing, terrifying,
earth-shattering. This pregnancy had been all of these.

Anyone who has waited through seasons of joy,
of longing, or of sorrow can understand Israel's long
wait, often described in terms of labor pains. This is a
wait that has stretched across salvation history. A man
grows into a family. Twelve sons become twelve tribes.
The tribes become a nation. Prophets, judges, and kings
lead them. Everything presses on to one great event.

At times, the wait was exciting. Seas parted. Angels
visited. Walls tumbled. A donkey talked. At times, the
wait was difficult. Brothers argued. Kings failed. Generations were exiled. At times, the wait was terrifying.
People died. Nations fought. God was silent.

And then, he spoke.

With an angel's word, the wait comes to an end.
Three months later, a baby cries. And all of Ein Kerem

laughs. It is the birth of St. John the Baptist. The fore-runner has arrived.

Scripture is not clear about whether Mary remained with Elizabeth until right before John's birth or if she stayed until just after his birth. Many theologians think it is likely that Mary remained until Elizabeth's child was born. If so, Mary would have wiped away Elizabeth's tears when John the Baptist took his first breath. Mary would have been there to hold the final prophet who was promised in the last verses of the last chapter of the last book of the Old Testament: "Lo, I will send you Elijah, the prophet, before the day of the Lord comes" (Mal 3:23–24). She would have been there to laugh as they gazed upon the child who would proclaim *the Son*.

Mary knew the hour had come for her to return to Nazareth, to Joseph, and to her own final trimester that would culminate in the birth of a Savior. But first, she let her eyes fall upon the promised prophet. First, she shared a knowing glance with Elizabeth, and together, they praised God.

These two women know what we have come to know—that there is one response to a God who keeps his promises. There's only one thing left to do. It is time to give thanks and praise. It's what Hannah, Deborah, and Judith from the Old Testament have in common with Mary and Elizabeth. They all experienced a mighty work of the Lord, and, filled with a sense of wonder, they cried out to God in thanksgiving.

The final gift of the Visitation is the gift of thanksgiving.

Israel's days of anguished supplications have ended. God had heard and answered prayers—Israel's

prayers and also Elizabeth's prayers. It all flowed together—a nation's longing, an old woman's longing—and
life burst forth. One baby drew his first breath; the other
baby was the One who knit John together in Elizabeth's
womb. One child nursed at his mother's breast; the other
waited in the living tabernacle of Mary's womb. Elizabeth looked at her newborn son, and then she turned
her gaze toward Mary, whispering what would be on
the lips of any righteous woman in her place: "Thank
you. Thank you for saying yes to God. Thank you for
giving us a Savior. Thank you, because the whole world
will come to know what we know. God has visited his
people."

I don't know if Mary nodded, or bowed her head
meekly, or touched her own stomach in a prayer of
thanks. But I do know this: their song of joy became
a song of thanksgiving. In the first chapter of Luke's
Gospel, we read Zechariah and Mary's canticles. Both
are hymns of thanksgiving—set in Sacred Scripture like
bookends around the birth of St. John the Baptist. The
words of these two songs are words of thanksgiving to
the God who hears and answers prayers.

Every spiritual gift is meaningless if it does not
lead us to give God the glory. It is the purpose of all
creation—our most important reason for being. Hannah, Deborah, and Judith set the standard in the Old
Testament. Hannah's womb was opened, she bore a
son, and Samuel's birth prompted her to lift her song
of praise—Hannah's canticle. The people of Israel won
battles against their enemies, and for this reason Deborah and Judith lifted their songs of praise, their canticles.

Hannah's canticle in 1 Samuel is almost identical to Mary's Magnificat in St. Luke's Gospel. It is so similar that one can be confident that Mary knew it and that she used it as the starting point for her own song. "My heart exults in the LORD, my horn is exalted by my God. I have swallowed up my enemies; I rejoice in your victory" (see 1 Sm 2:1–10).

While Hannah's canticle is a beautiful foretaste of Mary's song, Mary's Magnificat is the quintessential song of praise to God. It is the ultimate canticle. This quiet, meek one—this young lady with bowed head— now lifts her face to God and sings. She proclaims. She leads the whole world in a chorus of praise to God. Here, we see a glimpse of the woman who will be crowned queen when her earthly pilgrimage ends. For just one moment, set aside the images you have in your head of a quiet, shy girl. Catch a glimpse of the radiant woman who is to reign at her Son's side. Listen now, as she sings:

> My soul proclaims the greatness of the Lord;
> my spirit rejoices in God my savior.
> For he has looked upon his handmaid's
>   lowliness;
> behold, from now on will all ages call me
>   blessed.
> The Mighty One has done great things for me,
> and holy is his name.
> His mercy is from age to age
> to those who fear him.
> He has shown might with his arm,
> dispersed the arrogant of mind and heart.
> He has thrown down the rulers from their
>   thrones

> but lifted up the lowly.
> The hungry he has filled with good things;
> the rich he has sent away empty.
> He has helped Israel his servant,
> remembering his mercy,
> according to his promise to our fathers,
> to Abraham and to his descendants forever.
>   (Lk 1:46–55)

We see all of the gifts at play in this canticle. If you have been praying the novena these last nine days (see appendix), you have sensed each gift in the words of the Magnificat. We hear Mary's *spontaneous* cries of praise as she proclaims *courageously* that God is worthy of honor and glory—not as one who sits in shadows, but as a woman who leads her people into the dawn of a new morning. The spirit of *joy* is in every line. She affirms her *readiness* to become part of the great Gospel story. Yet with a spirit of *humility* she calls herself a handmaid, magnifying *God's* greatness, letting *God* eclipse all. We see a glimpse in this canticle of her spirit of *adventure*— her willingness to receive the affection and gratitude of all generations for the sole purpose of leading every generation to her Son. We recognize her heart for *hospitality* as she turns the spotlight on the poor, the lowly, and the hungry. With a spirit of *wonder and awe* she captures for us this great thing that God has done, how he has fulfilled every promise to Israel, how he has triumphed over their enemies. Now, with a spirit of *thanksgiving*, the song spills forth for all generations.

Everything is ready for the Gospel story to reach the world and turn it upside down.

God has done great things for us. Holy is his name. The words catch fire in our hearts. It's contagious—this hymn of praise. Zechariah, who has not uttered a word in months, listened to Mary's song, and in the quiet of his heart, he began preparing his own canticle. And when the infant John is born, God opens Zechariah's mouth, and he announces the child's name. Then, he breaks the nine-month silence by singing a canticle of praise to God—and the words echo Mary's song. Yes, Mary's hymn of thanksgiving is contagious!

Zechariah's song rises from his heart because he has taken Mary into his home and learned from her. His song flows from hers even as her song flows from Hannah's song of old. Listen, and be swept away by the metaphors embedded in the lyrics: a horn of salvation, a daybreak from on high, an oath fulfilled, a path of peace.

We can almost imagine Elizabeth and Mary's faces as they listened. Did they look at one another with knowing glances and overflowing hearts? Did tears run down their faces?

Mary listened carefully. So carefully that she was able to share Zechariah's song with the early Church decades later:

> Blessed be the Lord, the God of Israel,
>   for he has visited and brought redemption to
>   his people.
> He has raised up a horn for our salvation
>   within the house of David his servant,
>   even as he promised through the mouth of his
>   holy prophets from of old:
> salvation from our enemies and from the hand
>   of all who hate us,

to show mercy to our fathers
and to be mindful of his holy covenant
and of the oath he swore to Abraham our
    father,
and to grant us that,
rescued from the hand of enemies,
without fear we might worship him
in holiness and righteousness
before him all our days.
And you, child, will be called prophet of the
    Most High,
for you will go before the Lord to prepare his
    ways,
to give his people knowledge of salvation
through the forgiveness of their sins,
because of the tender mercy of our God
by which the daybreak from on high will visit
    us
to shine on those who sit in darkness and
    death's shadow,
to guide our feet into the path of peace.
    (Lk 1:67–79)

Like Mary's Magnificat, Zechariah's song also con-
tains hints of the gifts we have talked about. It serves
as an invitation to us, to go and do likewise—to receive
what we hear and see and to lift our own song of praise.
What is the canticle in your heart? How does it go?
Which gifts are at play in your song?

You have a song to sing and the world longs to
hear it.

When we stand and sing, when we lift high the
name of our God, when we give thanks and praise,

others witness our joy, courage, spontaneity, humility—
all of it. It draws them in.

You have experienced the outpouring of the Holy
Spirit as you studied the gifts, and now God is calling you to action. Mary received him—and you have
received him. She was filled with joy, a joy that propelled
her to go and share the Good News. Let the joy of the
Lord fill you, strengthen you, and send you out. Yes,
you have received him—for he is the Eucharist. Can you
guess what the word *Eucharist* means? *Thanksgiving*. It
means thanksgiving! Let us go out and share—with a
spirit of thanksgiving.

All of Ein Kerem joined in the song of praise, and
those around us will join in the song—if we are willing to lead them. Every Catholic who receives the Most
Blessed Sacrament receives Jesus Christ; and everyone
who receives the Eucharist is sent out to share Christ
with the world. The Eucharist—*thanksgiving*—propels
us outside of ourselves, to find the Elizabeths and Zech-
ariahs of our world.

This is how we express the gift of thanksgiving.
It is a gift we receive from God. And then we go out to
share that gift.

Every gift you have been given is a gift from God.
And every gift is meant to be shared. That is how you
become a Christ-bearer.

Mary reveals the two doors that lead to a spirit
of thanksgiving. The first is to meditate upon the One
we have received: God, Lord, Creator. The One who
flung the stars into space and formed every valley and
mountain, the One who holds all things in his hands—
he became so small and humble, that you have been

given the opportunity to rise from your knees, walk the aisle, bow, and take him into your own body. A spirit of thanksgiving is waiting to fill you when Christ comes to you in the Eucharist.

The second door to thanksgiving is to meditate upon what the Lord has done for us. Consider his passion and death—our only hope for eternal life. This Holy One of Israel is making us holy. He is fitting us for heaven. He is saving us. He has freed us to live the abundant life in Christ. Now you have been marked with the Sign of the Cross and sealed with the Holy Spirit. You were sentenced to die, but now, the doors of life have been thrown open to you! Let us give thanks and praise to the Lord of Life.

On March 21, 2004, I was with my family at a restaurant, and I choked on a piece of food. I knew instantly that this was very bad. I couldn't speak, I couldn't breathe, and I couldn't cough. I looked up at my husband and pointed to my throat. He saw the terror in my eyes. My mother was sitting across from me and, horrified, said the words I wanted to say, "She can't breathe; oh, help her, she can't breathe."

Within seconds, my husband turned me around in my chair and began doing the Heimlich maneuver. There is something very horrible about knowing your life is being snuffed out and you have no other hope of reversing that process—except for complete reliance on your husband's vague understanding of the Heimlich maneuver. There are few things scarier than realizing you will die, right here, right now, if this doesn't work.

My husband attempted the procedure. And it didn't work. He tried again, and again. It wasn't working. He kicked the chair out from under me and stood me up. I had no strength, no thought, except, *I can't breathe!* John tried the procedure standing up. Again, nothing. I fumbled to put his hands in the right place. That thing that had to happen—my diaphragm being compressed to drive the air out of my lungs and the food out of my throat—it just wasn't happening.

That's when I realized this might not work at all. I realized that I was probably about to die. How many times had he tried? Five? Six? *Put your hands here, here!* My life depended upon communicating without words.

I could tell that I was about to pass out. The room became dark. And then, the piece of food that was lodged in my throat shifted position, and air rushed in suddenly. I wasn't going to die that day after all.

John and I collapsed into the chairs.

The entire restaurant was staring at us, hundreds of people holding their breath with me, now exhaling a collective sigh of relief. John saved me.

As the days went by, I wanted to tell everyone I met not to give up if they are ever choking. The maneuver may take much effort. You may think you are dying. And then, life-breath rushes in again. You stand with shaky legs, knowing what almost happened. Thanksgiving fills you. You know how close to the edge you were. You can barely speak of it. And yet, you must speak of it. You must tell others, to let them know what you fumbled through and found: the *way* to go about it, the *truth* about its efficacy, the *life* it saves.

Yes, the way, the truth, and the life.

We have forgotten what is at stake. To grasp what Mary has done for us in giving us our Redeemer, we

must try to imagine eternity without God. Only then
can we begin to understand the gift we have in Christ,
our only hope for salvation. Only then can we whisper a
word of thanksgiving to Mary, as Elizabeth once did—to
Christ, as Mary teaches us to do.

Their songs and our songs burst forth. How can
we remain silent? How can we know that we have
Christ and not share that Good News? It should propel
us down the road and into the highways and byways,
through mountains and river valleys—as it did Mary.

It should free our tongues to speak, to sing, to
shout. "Arise. Shine. For your light has come. And the
glory of the Lord has risen upon you!" (Is 61:1). Now,
go and tell the world about it!

ℛEFLECTION

What gifts have I been given? If I believe they are truly
given to me by God, how does that realization affect
me? Do I receive the Eucharist with a spirit of thanksgiving? Do I receive him with the hope of being strength-
ened enough to share him with others? Have I become
the Christ-bearer that Mary and Elizabeth want me to
become? Are there people in my life who need to know
this Savior or perhaps just need to be reminded that he
loves them? How can I let my gratitude overflow and
touch their lives?

Lord, give me a spirit of thanksgiving. You are the ultimate gift, and I want to share you with those I love. Help me to do that. Help me to become creative in how I share you—to find ways of sharing you that speak to the hearts of others and that help them to see you and to respond. Change me, so that I reflect the Christ-bearing models I have in Mary and Elizabeth. For your glory. Amen.

CHAPTER TEN

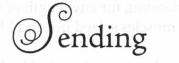

$\mathscr{S}$ending

In May, 2014, I traveled to Israel with the Catholic Press Association as a guest of the Israel Ministry of Tourism to cover the Holy Father's meeting with Bartholomew I, the Patriarch of Constantinople, in Jerusalem. Our pilgrimage began in Nazareth and ended nine days later in Ein Kerem. I have never walked so far, and certainly not over such rugged terrain, as I did during those nine days.

It became a kind of novena, a prayerful journey. My mind began to grasp what it was like for Mary to travel through those hills and along that Jordan River Valley. It was hot. And she would have relied upon the springs to sustain her. It was long. And her feet would have ached. It was unpredictable. And she would have had to trust the Lord fully. It was beautiful. And she would have been filled with more and more wonder and awe as she journeyed south to Elizabeth and Zechariah's home.

Our team was quick to find shade wherever shade could be found. We went through countless refills of our water bottles and had ravenous appetites every evening after walking and climbing and standing. My ankles swelled up just as they did when I was pregnant. I had a hard time standing for any length of time. But if I sat too long, my muscles seized up, and I had to work out the kinks.

We had a phenomenal guide. He showed us places and made connections between the Old Testament and the New Testament. This was his homeland, and he knew it just as one knows the layout of his own home. Our guide led, and we followed—as the Lord once led Mary and helped her connect the old to what was being made new, as the Lord kept her safe, and as the Lord made a way for her through some of the most rugged hills on the planet.

It had been an amazing journey traveling from Galilee to Judea. There were palm trees, olive trees, hills, banana trees, and pomegranate trees. Breezes were cool and refreshing, while the piercing sun burned the skin and dehydrated the body. Lizards perched on rocks. There were seas, rivers, and underground springs that burst forth to the surface. Caves and nooks were in the rocky heights where bandits might hide—or where a girl might pause to step into the shade. Old and new mingled.

On the first day of our journey, we encountered Nazareth and saw the place where Archangel Gabriel spoke words to Mary that changed her world and ours. From Nazareth, we traveled throughout Galilee and eventually to Jerusalem and to Ein Kerem, just a few miles from the Holy City. What a blessing, to be able to visit Ein Kerem, nestled among the hills of Judea, where Mary stayed with Elizabeth.

During my nine-day journey from Nazareth to Ein Kerem, I saw the landscape Mary saw. Leaving her home in Nazareth, where the Word of God was made flesh within her womb, I saw Mount Tabor in the distance. We drove past Jezreel, a fertile valley that Sacred Scripture designates as the Valley of Armageddon. From there, Mary would have chosen to traverse the hills or to take the path along the Jordan River Valley. The first would be dangerous, a perfect hiding place for bandits and a road that cuts through Samaria with its host of troubles. But if it had been summer, the heat may have forced her into the higher elevations where breezes come like bits of grace at just the right moment. Eventually she would have passed Jacob's well and crossed the road to Jericho where the Israelites of old marched around city walls at God's direction and the walls fell down. She might have thought of a woman named Rahab who hid the Israelite spies and so was spared when the walls fell. She may have smiled as she walked, remembering how Rahab married one of those spies and became the mother to Boaz, how Boaz married a Moabite named Ruth, and how Ruth became the grandmother to Jesse and the great-grandmother to David. As she walked, perhaps she pondered the lineage that led to her Son, this one who would inherit David's throne—this little life, now growing within her.

If she traveled along the Jordan, she may have washed her feet in the river. And as she passed Jerusalem, she would have thought of King David and had a view of the Temple Mount. She may have touched the walls of the city as she passed—perhaps even the Western Wall, which is all that remains of the city David knew. Somewhere within those walls, in the heart of Mount Zion, was David's tomb. And here, now, within her, was David's promised descendant. The journey was almost over. What had it been? Four days? Five? Even more? The distance was more than eighty miles and thousands upon thousands of steps.

But just a few miles from Jerusalem, over some of the most beautiful tree-dotted hills, Mary would have encountered Ein Kerem.

That final climb is hard. My eyes took in the hills. My soul magnified a God who would see fit to invite me to come to this spot—a little girl from Iowa, a preacher's daughter who did not know Mary as a mother until a late-in-life conversion, a little sister to all the others, perhaps the smallest, the least likely. And yet, Mary had beckoned to me, saying: "Come. Let me show you Elizabeth's home." I whispered to Mary as I descended the hill of the Visitation: "There's not nearly enough time in Ein Kerem, not nearly enough." And I knew that is how Mary had felt at the end of those three months—a visit so precious, a visit so fleeting.

"But I cannot remain in Ein Kerem forever. There are more people who need to meet Jesus." These were Mary's thoughts; these were my thoughts.

We made a brief stop at St. John the Baptist Church before leaving Ein Kerem. I saw Zechariah's canticle written on the walls in many languages in the same manner that Mary's Magnificat is written on the walls that surround the Church of the Visitation. And I smiled. Yes, Zechariah must have heard Mary's song. He had followed her spontaneous canticle with one of his own—like an echo, passing through these hills and touching the world beyond.

I thought again of Mary, how she must have had an all-too-brief moment with the infant John. And off she went, back to her home.

This was not the end. It was just the beginning. But it was time to leave Ein Kerem.

This is where the Gospel was first shared, one person to another. It is the place where true spiritual friendship was born. It is the place where lives were touched, a baby leaped, an old woman cried out for joy. This is where Archangel Gabriel's words were repeated for the first time beyond the gates of Nazareth.

The Messiah has come. Soon the rest of the world would know. But the secret had been theirs for just a moment of time. All that lay before them, everything in those hills and beyond—it all waited for this little one. He would change the course of history and fulfill all that the Law and prophets had said.

He was the reason for all of it: for Abraham, Isaac, Jacob, David, a parting sea, the Ark of the Covenant, the falling walls of Jericho. He was the reason that a

Moabite is remembered, that the Israelites were rescued from slavery, that a nation returned from exile. He was the reason that the Temple was built, that an angel appeared, that a prophet called down fire and called the people to turn to God. And now, in the hidden place of his Mother's womb, he grew.

A virgin's fingers touched the mezuzah on Elizabeth's doorpost; her mind paused to remember the Shema; and her tiny foot crossed the threshold at Ein Kerem as a voice announced the Gospel message. *Elizabeth, your Savior has visited you. And you are standing on holy ground.* Indeed, people from lands yet to be discovered would one day cross the ocean just to see this place because the Gospel message was first preached here. The Messiah journeyed here first by way of his mother.

And you, Elizabeth, are the first to receive the Good News—and in turn to proclaim it. You are the first to believe by way of a human voice. You are the embodiment of the Old Covenant, and you carry within you the forerunner to the Messiah. Arise. Go to the one who calls your name. Embrace her, for she has visited you this day with a message from the Lord.

For the Lord who is mighty has done great things. And holy is his name.

I stood at Ein Kerem, and my soul was so full that the tears came and ran down my face. I looked up at the Visitation steeple that reaches into the sky, and I remembered.

Nothing can stand in our way—no mountain, no heat, no rock, no bandit, not the length of the journey, not the doubt of those we've left behind, not the lateness of the hour, not the fragility of the human body, neither height, nor depth, nor anything else in all creation. Nothing stands in the way of the advancing Gospel story.

The message of Christ is given to be shared. He visits others by way of our own feet, by way of our own hands, by way of our own voices. By going, we give birth to Jesus Christ. We tell others as Mary told Elizabeth. Yes, Elizabeth awaits—the Elizabeth that you alone can visit. The hills of Judea must be crossed—and the hills are in your own backyard. So go, spread the Good News.

The Blessed Mother gently tells us that we are ready. It's time to share Christ with the same kind of deliberateness in our efforts that Mary had as she traveled to Elizabeth's home.

You may feel as if you do not know where to begin. You may feel it's as if you are being asked to walk on water, and you just aren't made for that. The truth is you were made for that. Yes, you will need spontaneity, and the years may have destroyed all desire to act spontaneously. You will need courage, and the experiences you've had may have stolen every courageous urge you once had. You will need to lean in to joy, and perhaps you haven't felt joy for a very long time. You will need to accept whatever comes next, and perhaps you have planned everything in your life for as long as you can remember. You will need to take on humility, even if your tongue sometimes has a way of betraying you, of letting the world know that you are neither humble nor meek. And you may feel as though you are short on every other gift listed in these chapters as well.

But turn your eyes to Mary and Elizabeth, and realize that age and social status and family opinion and educational achievement have nothing to do with it. God can infuse you with each and every gift necessary for the work of bringing Christ to others. It doesn't matter if you are a woman or a man, a young person or a senior citizen, highly educated or barely able to read the words in this book. It doesn't matter if you work on Wall Street or live down a country lane. It doesn't even matter if you are the only one in your family who still practices the faith. The only necessary prerequisite is that you come before our Lord with a willing heart. It is the prerequisite you read about in the introduction. You must be open to whatever God wants to do with you and through you. It is your *fiat*—your *let it be done unto me according to your word.*

Through Baptism, you have been called to share the Gospel message, to become a missionary in your corner of the world. This is the work we are called to: to share what we have received, *who* we have received! For you, the Annunciation has already taken place. Through the Sacrament of Holy Communion, Christ has come to *you.* Every time you receive the Eucharist, you become a living tabernacle. And then you are commanded to go and share the Good News! Even the word *Mass* is a kind of mandate because the word means "the sending." You have been sent.

Where is God sending you? Mary shared Christ with Elizabeth and Zechariah. But when she returned to Nazareth, she didn't keep Christ to herself. She continued to share him—with Joseph, with Bethlehem, with Egypt, with Nazareth, with Jerusalem, and with the entire world.

Yes, you are ready to bear Jesus Christ to your world for the glory of God. So invite someone to Mass. Write a letter. Make a dessert. Throw open the door of your guest room for a grandchild, a godchild, a stranger. Send a holy card or a spiritual book to an old friend or a family member. Visit the adoration chapel. Whatever it is that God is asking of you, do it all—but model everything you do after Mary.

> Mary, Virgin and Mother, you who, moved by the Holy Spirit, welcomed the word of life in the depths of your humble faith: as you gave yourself completely to the Eternal One, help us to say our own "yes" to the urgent call, as pressing as ever, to proclaim the good news of Jesus. Filled with Christ's presence, you brought joy to John the Baptist, making him exult in the womb of his mother. . . . Mother of the living Gospel, wellspring of happiness for God's little ones, pray for us.[1]
>
> —Pope Francis

Appendix of Prayers

NOVENA

This novena is a prayer to become a bearer of Christ to the world.

Begin each day with the Act of Consecration to Jesus, the Shema, and the Magnificat, followed by an Our Father, Hail Mary, and Glory Be.

Act of Consecration:

I offer myself to you, Son of the Most High God, to become a Christ-bearer to all those I encounter—my family, friends, community, country, world—for the sake of the kingdom of God. May your Blessed Mother become a model for me of holiness and mission. I desire to be open to the movement of the Holy Spirit and to welcome each of the gifts of the Visitation—especially the gift of (*insert name of today's gift here*)—for the glory of God the Father, the outpouring of the Holy Spirit, and the ministry of our Lord and Redeemer, Jesus Christ. Holy Mother of God, journey with me. St. Elizabeth, teach me to be ready to receive a visitation from the Lord—and to be open to whatever God may ask of me.

139

Pray the Shema with a focus on today's gift:

$\mathscr{H}$ear, O Israel, the Lord is our God, the Lord is
one. You shall love the Lord, your God, with all
your heart, with all your soul, and with all your
resources. And these things that I command you
today shall be upon your heart. And you shall
teach them to your children, and you shall speak
of them when you sit in your house and when
you go on the way, when you lie down and when
you rise up. And you shall bind them as a sign
upon your arm and they shall be an ornament
between your eyes. And you shall write them
upon the doorposts of your house and on your
gates. (Dt 6:4–9)

Mary's Magnificat:

$\mathscr{M}$y soul proclaims the greatness of the
    Lord;
my spirit rejoices in God my savior.
For he has looked upon his handmaid's
    lowliness;
behold, from now on will all ages call me
    blessed.
The Mighty One has done great things for me,
and holy is his name.
His mercy is from age to age
to those who fear him.
He has shown might with his arm,
dispersed the arrogant of mind and heart.
He has thrown down the rulers from their
    thrones

but lifted up the lowly.
The hungry he has filled with good things;
the rich he has sent away empty.
He has helped Israel his servant,
remembering his mercy,
according to his promise to our fathers,
to Abraham and to his descendants forever.
(Lk 1:46–55)

Our Father . . .
Hail Mary . . .
Glory be . . .
Amen.

Acknowledgments

Since 2004, Mary Beth Kremski and I have experienced a divine visitation. Without Mary Beth, I could not have written this book. She possesses each of these gifts in abundance, and I am the beneficiary of the Holy Spirit's gifts active in her life. I am humbled to know that she has experienced that same divine visitation through me.

I would also like to thank my parents, who introduced me to Christ when I was a child. Truthfully, I had a concept of God's existence even before I fully had a sense of my own identity. There is no greater gift a parent can give a child.

I am indebted to Shawn Mueller, my RCIA instructor; to Fr. Tom Miller, my parish priest, confessor, and spiritual director; to the Visitation Sisters in St. Louis, Missouri, especially Sr. Marie Therese Ruthmann; to Jill Daly and the Israel Ministry of Tourism and to tour guide Ron Harari; and to Lil Copan, my editor at Ave Maria Press. Each one is a dear friend and gift from God.

And finally, I am thankful for John Bossert, my husband, friend, and tech support. God knew what he was doing when he placed us both in graduate school at the same time. John, thanks for taking my hand—and for never letting go.

May 31, 2014
Feast of the Visitation of the Blessed Virgin Mary

Notes

Introduction: Openess to the Holy Spirit

1. Francis, *General Audience*, November 6, 2013.
2. Cardinal Ratzinger, *Mary, the Church at the Source* (San Francisco: Ignatius Press, 2005), 61.
3. Michael E. Gaitley, MIC, *33 Days to Morning Glory* (Stockbridge, MA: Marian Press, 2011), 50.
4. Louis de Montfort, *True Devotion to the Blessed Virgin* (Bay Shore, NY: Montfort Publications, 1996), 104.

2. A Spirit of Courage

1. George Weigel, *Evangelical Catholicism* (New York: Basic Books, 2013), 82.

3. A Spirit of Joy

1. Edward Sri, *Walking With Mary* (New York: Image, 2013), 70.
2. Francis, *Evangelii Gaudium*, 272.
3. John F. Doerfler, *Mass of Ordination and Installation in the Diocese of Marquette*, February 11, 2014.

4. A Spirit of Readiness

1. Donald Wuerl, *New Evangelization: Passing on the Catholic Faith Today* (Huntington, IN: Our Sunday Visitor, 2013), 86–87.
2. Marge Fenelon, *Imitating Mary: Ten Marian Virtues for the Modern Mom*, CatholicMom.com Books (Notre Dame, IN: Ave Maria Press, Inc., 2013), 44.

3. Francis, "A Woman Against the Tide," May 31, 2013.

4. Kelly Wahlquist, *Catholic Women for Christ* presentation, St. Louis, January 25, 2014.

6. A Spirit of Adventure

1. George Weigel, *Evangelical Catholicism* (New York: Basic Books, 2013), 80.

2. John Paul II, *Redemptoris Missio*, 3.

7. A Spirit of Hospitality

1. Cardinal Carlo Maria Martini, *The Gospel Way of Mary* (Frederick, MD: Word Among Us Press, 2011), 24.

10. Sending

1. Francis, *Evangelii Gaudium*, 288.

Denise Bossert earned a bachelor of arts in English education, magna cum laude, at the University of Dubuque in 1989. In 2001, she was awarded a master of arts in literature from Southern Illinois University at Edwardsville. Bossert also studied theology at the Paul VI Institute in St. Louis. She has taught literature at the primary, secondary, and college levels and has worked as a religious education coordinator and Confirmation assistant.

The daughter and former wife of Protestant ministers, Bossert converted to the Catholic Church in 2005 after being inspired by the books of St. John of the Cross and St. Teresa of Avila. She writes a syndicated column called *Catholic by Grace* for diocesan newspapers across the United States. She has also written for *Canticle Magazine* (now called *Women of Grace*), *Women for Faith and Family*, and *Catholic Exchange*.

Bossert is a member of the Legion of Mary, Catholic Writers Guild, and ACTS Retreat Community. She has appeared on a variety of television and radio shows, including EWTN's Journey Home and *Women of Grace*, the *Son Rise Morning Show*, *Catholic Vitamins, On Call*, and *Seize the Day*. She gives talks at parishes and to women's groups on conversion, women of salvation history, and spiritual mentoring. Denise and her husband, John, have four children and five grandchildren and live in New Melle, Missouri.